CIVIL WAR WORDBOOK

CIVIL WAR WORDBOOK

including Sayings, Phrases and Slang

Darryl Lyman

COMBINED BOOKS
Pennsylvania

PUBLISHER'S NOTE

Combined Books, Inc., is dedicated to publishing books of distinction in history and military history. We are proud of the quality of writing and the quantity of information found in our books. Our books are manufactured with style and durability and are printed on acid-free paper. We like to think of our books as soldiers: not infantry grunts, but well dressed and well equipped avant garde. Our logo reflects our commitment to the modern and yet historic art of bookmaking.

We would like to hear from our readers and invite you to write to us at our offices in Pennsylvania with your reactions, queries, comments, even complaints. All of your correspondence will be answered directly by a member of the Editorial Board or by the author.

For information, address:
COMBINED BOOKS, INC.
151 East 10th Avenue
Conshohocken, PA 19428

Library of Congress Cataloging-in-Publication Data
Lyman, Darryl, 1944-
Civil War wordbook : including sayings, phrases, and slang / Darryl Lyman
p.   cm.
Includes bibliographical references.
 ISBN 0-938289-25-X :
 1. United States—History—Civil War, 1861-1865—Dictionaries. I, Title
E468.9.L96   1993
973.7'O3—dc20   93-30111

Combined Books Edition   1 2 3 4 5

First published in the USA in 1993 by Combined Books and distributed in North America by Stackpole Books, 5067 Ritter Road, Mechanicsburg, PA 17055 and internationally by Greenhill Books, Park House, 1 Russell Gardens, London NW119 NN.

Printed in the United States of America.

Introduction

Civil War Wordbook is a compilation of hundreds of expressions that reflect the time and the people of the American Civil War. Entries fall into three broad categories: general language of the era, standard military terms, and soldiers' or sailors' lingo. Sometimes the categories overlap.

The language of the era includes the names of Civil War-related organizations, such as *ladies' gunboat society* and *Sanitary Commission*; civilian groups or types, such as *Committee on the Conduct of the War* and *lame duck*; political acts and symbols, such as *Proclamation of Thanksgiving* and *Stars and Bars*; services or objects resulting from new postal regulations, such as *first class* and *soldier's letter*; money, such as *greenback* and *shucks*; and items that fused postal and monetary purposes, such as *encased postage stamp* and *postage currency*.

Many terms of common usage had a directly military origin. People spoke of a *blockade-runner*, a *bounty jumper*, and a *draftee*. And everyone knew about the *ironclad* ships, the *Medal of Honor*, and the *Thanks of Congress*.

Standard military terms include the names of weapons, such as *Gatling gun*; ammunition, such as *Minié ball*; uniform accessories, such as *havelock*; communication systems, such as the *Beardslee Telegraph*; and many others, such as *color-bearer*, *desiccated vegetables*, *haversack*, *partisan ranger*, and *Veteran Reserve Corps*. The Civil War also saw the creation of some new American ranks, notably *admiral*, *commodore*, and *ensign*.

Civil War soldiers' lingo constitutes one of America's richest, most colorful language legacies. One of the soldiers' favorite patterns was to apply an official word or phrase in a completely unexpected, and sometimes hilarious, way. *Brevet*, to *fire and fall back*, to *flank*, and *shoulder strap* all received that treatment.

Many expressions reflect the rural background of most Civil War soldiers. *Beehive* (knapsack), *gone up* (hopeless), *Here's your mule* (we've been here), and *weevil fodder* (hardtack) are examples.

Soldiers used colorful terms for various weapons: *coffee-mill gun*, *pumpkin slinger*, and *Yankee seven-devils*, to name a few. They called their equipment *dog tent*, *horse collar*, *patent bureau*, and so on. Some uniform ornaments went by the terms *chicken guts* and *sardine box*. Soldiers loved to name their footwear: *crooked shoe*, *ferryboat*, *whang*.

Both armies battled the body louse, known as a *body-guard*, a *crumb*, and a *grayback*, as well as diarrhea and dysentery, called the *quickstep* and the *evacuation of Corinth*, among other names. Sarcasm and complaining were prevalent: *all in the three years*; *rich man's war, poor man's fight*; *Who wouldn't be a soldier?*

Food was a favorite topic, and the soldiers' slang terms said much about their opinions of it: *baled hay*, *hellfire stew*, *desecrated vegetables*, *embalmed beef*, *sanitary fodder*, *sheet-iron cracker*, *son of a seadog*, *worm castle*. A cook was a *dog robber*. Whiskey was called *busthead, dead shot, how come you so, knock-'em-stiff, rifle knock-knee, rotgut,* and *tarantula juice.*

To visit a brothel was *to go down the line.* Related terms included *fancy lady, madam,* and *parlor house.*

Personal names spawned many terms, such as *to butlerize, Jeff Davis box, Lincoln rifle,* and *Sherman's hairpin.* Epithets abounded: *bummer, buttermilk ranger, doughboy, galvanized Yankee, hospital rat, mossyback, $300 man, webfoot.* A doctor was *loose bowels* or *opium pills.*

Civil War sailors contributed comparatively little to the American language, probably because so many of them were foreigners. However, sailors' lingo did include many nicknames for recently developed vessels, like *cheesebox* and *Pook turtles,* and for new weapons, such as *devil fish* and *soda-pop gun.*

Inclusions and Exclusions

Expressions selected for inclusion in *Civil War Wordbook* were popularized during, and were in some way related to, the Civil War. Exceptions are noted in the text. Excluded are technical terms (e.g., weapon components) and individualisms (e.g., *squashmolished,* "hung over"), because they did not, and do not, have a general audience. Also excluded, because they are already well covered in many other books, are names and nicknames of songs, persons, battles, military units, and geographical locations (e.g., battlefields). The few exceptions are noted in the text.

How to Read the Entries

A typical entry consists of the term, variant forms (if any), the definition, the origin, and cross-references (if any). Modern spellings are used for the entry headings. Cross-references serve the following purposes:

aka: The other term has basically the same meaning.

cf.: The other term has a different, but related, meaning.

q.v.: The other term helps in the definition of the entry term.

Same...as (q.v.): The entry term is defined under a term with the same meaning.

See: The entry term is alphabetized under another letter, or the entry term is defined under a term with a different meaning.

See also: The other term provides additional information on the entry term.

Abbreviations

aka: also known as

c.: about

cf.: compare

C.S.S.: Confederate States ship

e.g.: for example

i.e.: that is

q.v.: which see

U.S.S.: United States ship

Cross-references are intended to be useful to the reader, but, to avoid excess, not all possible cross-references have been listed.

CIVIL WAR WORDBOOK

A

abatis: A defensive obstacle formed of felled trees with sharpened branches pointing toward the enemy. The word was borrowed from French *abatis* ("mass of things thrown down") and used in English since the mid-1700s.

abolition soldiers (abolition soldiery): Union troops.

acoustic shadow: A phenomenon in which the sounds of battle cannot be heard by people nearby, but are clearly audible many miles away. Pockets of silence are created by a variety of factors, such as thick woods and unusual atmospheric conditions. Aka *silent battle*.

Adams hand grenade: A type of hand grenade patented in early 1865 by the North's John S. Adams. The grenade thrower wore a wrist strap attached to the priming pin; when he threw the grenade, the strap pulled the pin from the shell to ignite a fuse. However, if the pin did not emerge smoothly, the live grenade could easily end up at the thrower's own feet.

admiral: A naval officer of the highest rank, equivalent to an army general. The title had been used in England since the fifteenth century. However, before the Civil War the highest official rank in the American navy was captain, the small number of United States warships not justifying any higher title. With the war and the naval buildup came the Union's official creation of the ranks of *rear admiral* in 1862 and *vice admiral* in 1864. The rank of full *admiral* was not adopted till 1866, but during the Civil War the word was often applied to David Farragut (America's first vice admiral and full admiral).

Ager gun: A single-barreled weapon operated by turning a crank that dropped cartridges from a hopper into a revolving cylinder. Invented by Wilson Ager. Aka *coffee-mill gun* (because it resembled a coffee grinder), *Union repeating gun* (because of its rapid fire), and simply *Union gun*.

agnew: A type of attire worn by Sanitary Commission nurses. It was a man's army shirt (the prototype was borrowed from a doctor named Agnew)—with the collar open, the sleeves rolled up, and the shirttails out—worn over a full skirt without hoops.

alert club: An organization of Northern children who collected food and money to help the Union soldiers. Many communities had alert clubs.

all in the three years: A Union soldiers' expression meaning "all the same to the average soldier," whose term of service, among the users of the phrase, was scheduled for three years. Typically uttered when something went wrong.

all quiet on the Potomac (all quiet along the Potomac): A common saying among Northerners early in the war, a sarcastic reference to official telegrams describing a military quietude that many people regarded as an intolerable delay by General McClellan. Late in 1861, *Harper's Weekly* published a poem by Ethel Lynn Beers, "The Picket Guard," which included the line "All quiet along the Potomac to-night."

all right on the goose, to be: See *goose question*.

Ambulance Corps: An army unit officially created by the United States Congress in 1864. The term *ambulance corps* had been applied unofficially to medical groups since 1861.

American Letter Express Company: A postal service with special dispensation to deliver mail to both North and South. Founded in 1861 with offices in Louisville and Nashville, it existed only a few months before military conflicts halted the company's operations.

amnesty proclamation: A presidential proclamation granting pardon to certain categories of people who had participated in the rebellion. The term was especially used in reference to the *Proclamation of Amnesty and Reconstruction* (q.v.).

anaconda: (1) A derisive name for Winfield Scott's early plan to avoid war by blockading Southern ports, occupying positions along the Mississippi River, and "squeezing" the South till the crisis had passed. The term was coined by the radical Union press, who wanted a quick military victory. Journalists got the idea for the name from reports that George McClellan had called it a "boa-constrictor" plan. (The anaconda, like the boa constrictor, is a snake that kills by constriction.) Contemporary publications often printed the term in such forms as "great anaconda" and "anaconda theory," but eventually *Anaconda Plan* became standard. Aka *Union anaconda*. (2) Hence, the Northern army.

Anglo-Confederate: Pertaining to the English and the Southern Confederacy, as in "the Anglo-Confederate blockade-running steamer *Chatham*."

Anglo-Rebel: Pertaining to the forces of England and the Southern Confederacy, as in "the Anglo-Rebel navy."

ankle boot: A boot or shoe that rose to about the ankle. The ankle boot was similar to the *Jefferson boot* (q.v.), but the *ankle boot* had several eyelets for lacing, whereas the Jefferson had a single thong. The term *ankle boot* had been in use since at least the 1830s, especially among cavalrymen.

antebellum: Existing before a war. The word comes from Latin *ante bellum* ("before the war"). It was first popularized, and is still most commonly used, with reference to the Civil War. In 1862, for example, Mary Chestnut wrote in her diary about the "antebellum days."

anti-secession: Opposed to the secession of the Southern states from the Union.

anything to preserve the Union: A Yankee catchphrase expressing Federal determination to win the war.

ardent: Strong distilled liquor, especially in the phrase "the ardent." Civil War soldiers often used this expression, which goes back to at least the 1830s and is a variant of the older and more polite *ardent spirits*.

argee: Inferior whiskey. From *r.g.*, an abbreviation of *rotgut* (q.v.).

Arkansas toothpick: (1) During the Civil War, a popular name for a *side knife* (q.v.). (2) Since the 1820s or 1830s, a popular name for the *bowie knife* (q.v.).

Arlington National Cemetery: A final resting-place established by the United States government in 1864 in Arlington, Virginia. The land had once belonged to George Washington; later to his adopted son, G.W. Parke Custis; and then to Robert E. Lee (who had married a Custis).

army blue: The blue uniform worn by United States soldiers. The term seems to have been first recorded just before the beginning of the Civil War. See also *blue* (1).

army correspondent: A writer employed by a periodical to be with an army and to contribute war news.

army grayback: A louse. See also *grayback* (3).

Army of the Confederate States of America: The official name of the Confederate regulars, i.e., the permanent standing army. Aka (informally) *Confederate army* (q.v.),

Confederate States Army, and *Confederate States Regular Army*. However, this force was extremely small, and its chief function during the war was administrative. Most of the fighting was done by the volunteer forces known as the *Provisional Army of the Confederate States* (q.v.).

artificial oysters: A Southern dish consisting of grated corn mixed with egg and butter, rolled in batter, and fried in a pan.

A tent: A canvas tent with sides sloping downward from a ridgepole to the ground. So named because it looked somewhat like the letter A. Usually designed for four soldiers, but often holding more. Aka *wedge tent*, also for its shape.

avalanche: A soldiers' ironic misnaming of the unsafe two-wheeled ambulance that carried the wounded early in the war. In prewar Texas, *avalanche* had designated a spring wagon.

awkward squad: A group of soldiers who needed extra drill. The expression apparently originated in England in the late eighteenth century and then came to America in the early nineteenth. Civil War troops found plenty of use for the term.

A.W.O.L. (AWOL): An abbreviation for *absent without leave*. Some modern sources state that this abbreviation began during the Civil War. The earliest printed evidence, however, dates from World War I.

B

baled hay: A Union soldiers' term for *desiccated vegetables* (q.v.) because they included roots, leaves, and stalks.

barrel drill: A punishment in which the soldier had to stand on a barrel for a specified length of time, sometimes while holding a stick of wood or wearing a placard labeling the offender, such as "Thief."

barrel jacket (barrel overcoat, barrel shirt): A wooden barrel with holes made in the top, sides, and bottom for a man's head, arms, and legs, worn as a punishment by a soldier, sometimes with a placard attached stating the reason for this humiliation, such as "I stole my messmate's rations." This method of punishment originated long before the 1860s, but it was the Civil War that brought the treatment and the terms associated with it to widespread familiarity.

barricade, to: Same as *stockade, to* (q.v.).

Bars, The: Short for *Stars and Bars* (q.v.). Aka *Confederate Bars*.

baseball: An early form of the game that later came to be called America's "national pastime." Before the Civil War, baseball was an elitist game, known only to the Northern upper crust, particularly in the East. During the war, many Union soldiers encountered baseball for the first time, and it became their most popular competitive sport behind the lines.

battle correspondent: Same as *war correspondent* (q.v.).

battle flag: A *color* (q.v. [1]) carried into battle. Sometimes, especially in the Confederate army, a regimental flag separate from, and less formal than, the regiment's color. A Confederate battle flag was inscribed with the unit's battle honors, which in the Union army were listed on a *battle streamer* (q.v.).

Battle Flag, Confederate: The flag, approved by the War Department in 1861, to be flown in battle because the original flag so used, the *Stars and Bars* (q.v.), could not always be distinguished from the Union's Stars and Stripes. The Battle Flag is the flag still remembered and flown as *the* flag of the Confederacy. It consists of a red field with a blue Saint Andrew's cross on which are thirteen white stars. Often erroneously referred to as the Stars and Bars. See also *National Flag, Confederate*.

battle pin: A pin showing the battle(s) in which a soldier had served.

battle streamer: In Federal regiments, a streamer (a long narrow flag) attached to the staff of the unit's *color* (q.v. [1]) and bearing the names of the battles in which the unit had fought. In the South, battle honors were listed on a unit's *battle flag* (q.v.).

B.C.: A marking on containers of hardtack, probably standing for *Brigade Commissary* but interpreted by soldiers, poking fun at the apparent age of the crackers, as *Before Christ*.

Beardslee Telegraph: A portable telegraph system perfected by George W. Beardslee and used by Union forces during 1862-63. It eliminated the need for Morse code but had a limited range. Full name, Beardslee Patent Magneto-Electric Field Telegraph Machine. It was transported by a *Flying Telegraph Train* (q.v.).

beat: A loafer or sponger. The word was widely used among soldiers to designate a man who did not carry his weight. Probably from the slang verb *to beat* ("to cheat") as in "to beat someone out of money." *Deadbeat*, another word for a loafer or sponger, also came into vogue during the Civil War. The first syllable probably comes from the adjective *dead* ("complete"), as in "dead broke."

beaver: A name soldiers sometimes called each other because of their constant digging for cover. See also *gopher*.

Beecher's Bible: A Sharps rifle. So called because during the 1850s struggle over whether Kansas would become a free or slave state, the abolitionist Henry Ward Beecher said that slaveholders would understand a rifle better than they would a Bible, so he and his friends sent hundreds of Sharps rifles to the Free-Soilers in Kansas.

beehive: Soldiers' slang for a knapsack.

bell tent: Another name for the *Sibley tent* (q.v.), which was shaped somewhat like a bell. The term had been used in the eighteenth century for a different kind of tent.

belly band: A flannel bandage worn by soldiers who mistakenly believed that it would relieve dysentery.

Bermuda bacon: Pork bought by Northerners, salted, shipped to Bermuda, and then sold to the Confederacy.

big thing: A large, ambitious project. The expression originated among civilians before the Civil War; but during the war, soldiers gave it an ironic twist, often applying it to a bungled scheme.

Billy Yank: A Union soldier. The term was not widely used till after the war.

blackberry picker: A straggler. So named because after such a man lagged behind to avoid a march or a battle or to be intentionally captured (so that he could spend the rest of the war in the "safety" of a prison camp), he often claimed that he had simply stopped to pick fruit.

blackjack: Rum with molasses.

Black Republican: A contemptuous name in the South for a Republican friendly to the cause of Negro emancipation. The term was in use by at least the 1830s, but its greatest currency came during the Civil War and Reconstruction eras.

black snake: An abolitionist. Introduced as a retort to *copperhead* (q.v.), the term probably derives its adjective from *Black Republican*, while the noun corresponds to the "snake" sense of *copperhead*.

blenker, to: To steal. A term used by Northern soldiers after Union troops commanded by Louis Blenker had to raid farms to get supplies in Virginia in 1862.

blind shell: A shell with no powder, used for target practice.

blizzard: A volley of shots. Earlier the word had meant a single punch or shot. The "snowstorm" sense was not widely used till long after the war.

blockade: Illicit whiskey. A Southern term alluding to the "forbidden" nature of blockaded items, though the liquor itself was, of course, domestic moonshine.

blockade cotton: Cotton barred from foreign markets by Union blockades. Aka *Confederate cotton*.

blockade-run: The action of running a blockade.

blockade-runner: A vessel or person evading or attempting to evade a blockade.

blockade-running: The action of getting or attempting to get through a blockade.

blouse: A type of waist-length military coat worn for fatigue duty and field service. This sense of the word originated in America during the Civil War. *Blouse* had earlier, in England and France, designated a smocklike garment worn by workmen. After the Civil War, the word took on its more familiar modern sense of a loose-fitting upper garment for women.

blue: (1) The blue uniform of the United States Army. This sense of the word had been recorded since at least the 1840s. During the Civil War, it was used in such phrases as "Uncle Sam's blue." See also *army blue*. (2) A soldier in the Union army. So called, of course, because of his blue uniform. The word is often capitalized. (3) The North or its army. Commonly "the Blue." (4) A word used by Southerners in many disparaging references to Northerners. The origin of this use may be in the famous puritanical "blue laws" (so called either because they were printed on blue paper or because they were enforced with punishments resulting in blue bruises or dried blood) of colonial New England. *Bluenose*, for example, designated a New England prude by at least the early 1800s. For common Civil War examples see *bluebelly, bluebird, bluecoat,* and *blueskin*.

blueback: A piece of Confederate paper currency. So called because some important Richmond issues had blue backs. See also *Confed* (2), *grayback* (2), and *shucks*. Cf. *greenback*.

bluebelly: A Federal soldier. A Southern term of derision. It had been used as early as 1827 to mean a New Englander (see *blue* [4]), and by the 1850s a favorite form was *bluebellied Yankee*. At about the same time, the term was beginning to be applied to a United States soldier because of his blue uniform. During the Civil War, the two senses of *bluebelly*—Yankee and soldier—converged into a Southern epithet of particular vehemence.

bluebird: A Union soldier, whose "feathers" were blue.

bluecoat: A blue-uniformed Union soldier. The term was recorded by 1833 but not widely used till the Civil War.

blue cockade (cockade): A cockade (ornament on a hat) worn as a symbol of secession. South Carolinians initiated the practice in 1860, and later other Southerners imitated them. However, the blue cockade had, long before the Civil War, been an emblem of resistance in the South.

Blue Lodge: Same as *Sons of the South* (1) (q.v.).

Blue Mass: A fictitious religious service to which men on sick call were said to be going. So named by Union soldiers because a blue-colored pill (known as *blue mass*) was commonly prescribed by the medical staff.

blueskin: A Union soldier, especially in the West. The "skin," of course, was the uniform. In the eighteenth century, *blueskin* had meant a stern New Englander (see also *blue* [4]).

boarder: Same as *fancy lady* (q.v.).

boat battery: A heavily armed and armored vessel designed for bombarding purposes.

bodyguard: A Confederate soldiers' term for a louse, which roamed over a person's entire body. Cf. *Bragg's bodyguard*.

Bohemian: A newspaper reporter. The word had originally meant a native of Bohemia. Then it was applied to a Gypsy (because Gypsies were thought to have first entered western Europe through Bohemia), a gypsy of society (including a wandering literary artist), and finally a roving journalist during the Civil War.

Bohemian Brigade: Union war correspondents. A name they applied to themselves.

boiled hay: See *desiccated vegetables*.

bombproof: (1) (noun) A shelter from mortar and artillery attack. On the battlefield, there were two kinds: a quickly made shallow dugout, and a more elaborate structure with walls and a roof of logs and packed earth. Southern yards and gardens often had their own versions. The term had been so used since at least 1755, but the Civil War popularized the expression. (2) (noun) A person not exposed to battle. It was a derisive term applied not only to rear-echelon people, such as quartermasters and commissaries, but also to outright cowards, such as shirking soldiers and civilians who avoided military service. The place of safety occupied by such a person was also a bombproof. (3) (adjective) Resistant to bombs (a meaning used since the eighteenth century) or not exposed to the dangers of war, as in "bombproof editors."

Bonnie Blue Flag: The secession flag adopted by Mississippi in January 1861. It had a single white star on a blue field (a pattern used by other Southern states, such as Texas, long before the Civil War). The term was popularized through a song of the same name, written by Harry McCarthy, who witnessed the Mississippi secession convention and the unfurling of the new flag. The flag lasted only a few weeks, Mississippi adopting a variant of it with the blue field and white star in the upper left corner. Several other Southern states created their own versions of the Mississippi flag. The South Carolina flag, however, often erroneously mentioned as the *Bonnie Blue Flag*, had a blue field but no star (a defining element in the song, which gave birth to the term Bonnie Blue Flag).

bootee: An informal soldiers' term for a laced boot or shoe that rose to about the ankle. The term, a diminutive of *boot*, had been used since the late 1700s for a variety of civilian footwear.

bootleg: An artillery missile.

border free state: A state on the northern side of the border between North and South.

Border Ruffian: A member of proslavery Missouri gangs entering Kansas to intimidate Free-Soilers during the 1850s struggle over whether or not to make Kansas a slave state.

border slave state: A state on the southern side of the border between North and South.

Border Slave State Convention: A meeting of representatives from Southern and Western states held in Washington, D.C., in February 1861. The purpose was to bring the cotton states back into the Union and to avoid war. However, many states did not even bother to send representatives. The border states were the most active at the convention. Aka *Peace Conference* and *Peace Convention*.

bounty: A financial reward given to recruits to induce their entry into the army. Bounties, sometimes property, had been a long-standing military-naval tradition in England and America.

bounty broker: Someone who, for a commission, would induce a man to enlist in the army and then, typically, con the recruit out of much of his bounty. Bounty brokers dumped many unfit men into the service.

bounty fund: A sum of money provided for paying bounties to army enlistees. In the North, such funds were available through Federal, state, and local authorities, and a soldier might receive money from all three; in the South, recruits could generally count on only the Confederate government for a bounty.

bounty jumper: One who enlisted as a soldier to obtain a bounty and then deserted. Some men enlisted and deserted many times.

bounty jumping: The practice of enlisting to obtain a bounty and then deserting.

bowel complaint: A common euphemism among soldiers for diarrhea or dysentery.

bowie knife: (1) During the Civil War, a popular name for a *side knife* (q.v.). (2) Since the late 1820s, a kind of heavy hunting knife made famous by James Bowie. Aka *Arkansas toothpick* (q.v.).

boys in blue: Union soldiers, who wore a blue uniform. The term had been applied to British sailors in the eighteenth century and to American sailors by the early nineteenth.

boys in gray: Confederate soldiers, who wore a gray uniform.

Bragg's bodyguard (General Bragg's bodyguard): A Confederate soldiers' term for a louse. General Braxton Bragg was an unpopular Southern officer, noted for his strict discipline. Cf. *bodyguard*.

bread bag: A soldiers' term for a cloth or rubber *haversack* (q.v.). Before the war, the term had a long history of use in its simple sense as a container for bread.

Breadbasket of the Confederacy: The Shenandoah Valley, whose farms and mills served as the granary of the South.

Bread Riot: The April 2, 1863, public disturbance by a hungry crowd in Richmond, Virginia. The event began as a peaceful march toward bakeries to get loaves of bread.

Break rank, march!: The Civil War equivalent to the modern *Fall out!*

breastwork: A temporary chest-high protective earthwork over which a soldier could fire. The term had been in use since the 1600s.

Brecht tent: A combination tent, cloak, and bed, patented in 1862 by T.C. Brecht of the Northern army.

brevet: In the Union army, a commission giving an officer an honorary title higher than his officially listed rank. From French *brevet* ("brief letter," i.e., the document attesting to the commission), the English word had been so used since colonial times. Civil War soldiers, feeling that many brevet officers did not deserve their ranks, often gave the term a derisive connotation; see also *brevet horse* and *children by brevet*.

brevet hell: A battle.

brevet horse: Soldiers' slang for an army mule. Many ad hoc similar expressions were also used, such as *brevet turkey* for a turkey vulture.

brick: A block of *desiccated vegetables* (q.v.). Union troops coined the derisive term in reference to the thick, solid form of the dehydrated food.

bridle cutter: See *Joe Brown's pikes*.

bring a brick, to: To return to camp under the influence of liquor. This expression and its variants, such as *to have a brick in one's hat*, antedate the Civil War.

brogan: A civilian term applied by soldiers to a coarse army shoe, usually laced and ankle high. The word, an Irish Gaelic diminutive of the word for "shoe," had been in use since the early 1800s.

broker: Short for *bounty broker* (q.v.).

Brooke gun (Brooke rifle, Brooke rifled cannon): A Confederate heavy artillery piece invented by John Mercer Brooke. It was used on ironclads and in seacoast fortifications.

brought up to the bullring, to be: To be brought up for military punishment, especially execution.

buck, to: (1) The first step in *to buck and gag* (q.v.). (2) To bend (someone) across a log, preparatory to flogging.

buck and ball: A load consisting of three buckshot and a regular-size musket ball. Often used by Confederate soldiers who wielded caliber .69 muskets. The load and variants of the expression had been in use since the colonial period.

buck and gag, to: To punish by sitting the offender on the ground, drawing his knees up to his chin, wrapping his arms around his shins, tying his hands together, inserting a stick over his arms and under his knees, and gagging him (sometimes with a bayonet stuck into his mouth and secured there with strings tied around his head). This punishment, which over a period of time could become extremely painful, is said to go back to the American Revolutionary War.

buck the tiger, to: See *tiger*.

buffalo: A North Carolinian who favored the Union.

bullseye canteen: The model 1858 United States Army canteen with many concentric rings pressed into each side for added strength. Heavily produced from 1862 to 1865.

Bully for you!: Wonderful; good for you. The expression was a popular catchphrase during the war. *Bully*, in the sixteenth century, originally designated a loved or admired person; later, as an adjective, it meant fine or first-rate.

bully soup: Same as *panada* (q.v.). *Bully* here means good, first-rate.

bum: Probably short for *bummer* (q.v.). The modern senses of bum originated just before and during the Civil War: the adjective meaning worthless; the verb meaning to loaf, beg, or wander; and the noun meaning tramp, loafer, or sponger. The Civil War caused an explosion in the use of the word; the war uprooted many men and got them used to a wandering camp life.

bumblebee: A bullet. Soldiers' slang.

bummer: (1) A loafer or sponger. From German *Bummler* ("loafer"). This sense of the word originated just before the war, perhaps in the Far West. (2) During the war, an independent forager, especially a soldier who left his ranks and plundered, often as part of a raiding force. See also *Sherman's bummers*. (3) A person in the safe rear of an army, such as a cook, a shirker, or a member of the medical staff.

bummer's cap: The Union army's regulation fatigue or forage cap. The name reflected the popular association of the cap with *Sherman's bummers* (q.v.).

bummer's roost: A favorable spot in the rear of an army, peopled by cooks, medical personnel, shirkers, and other noncombatants. See also *bummer* (3).

bureau: Short for *patent bureau* (q.v.).

Bureau of Engraving and Printing (Engraving and Printing Bureau): A division of the United States Treasury Department, informally organized in 1862 to print the nation's first legal-tender paper currency. The bureau became a distinct entity within the department in 1864. A congressional act formally recognized the bureau in 1869.

Bureau of Refugees, Freedmen, and Abandoned Lands: See *Freedmen's Bureau*.

Burnside blouse: A loose-fitting blue *blouse* (q.v.) named after Ambrose E. Burnside, a Union officer.

Burnside carbine: A rifled shoulder firearm patented in 1856 by Ambrose E. Burnside. The weapon was much used by the Union during the war.

Burnside hat (Burnside pattern felt hat): A low-crowned modification of the *Hardee hat* (q.v.).

Burnside stew: Hardtack soaked in water and then fried in pork fat. Northern soldiers named the dish after their commander Ambrose E. Burnside. Aka *hellfire stew* (q.v. [2]), *hish and hash* (q.v. [2]), and *skillygalee* (q.v. [1] and [2]).

bushwhacker: (1) A Confederate who lurked in the woods (bushes) and carried on irregular warfare or engaged in plundering. As early as 1813, the adjective form *bushwhacking* had meant practicing guerrilla warfare. But it was the Civil War that made *bushwhacker* a common term. The word originally had referred to a backwoodsman, one who literally whacked bushes to get them out of the way (or, in an apparently later sense, pulled on riverbank bushes to move a boat). (2) A deserter or draft dodger who became an outlaw hiding in the bushes. (3) In some Union areas, notably Kentucky, a Rebel sympathizer.

busthead: Inferior, especially homemade, whiskey. A Southern term that was recorded by at least 1857 and was often used by Confederate soldiers during the war. The earlier expression *on a bust* meant "on a drinking spree."

bustskull: Same as *busthead* (q.v.).

butcher's bill: A sarcastic term for a list of casualties.

butlerize, to: To steal. The verb refers to the Union's Benjamin F. Butler, who, while commanding in occupied New Orleans, was suspected of theft.

Butler Medal: An award given by the Union commander Benjamin F. Butler to the black troops of the XXV Corps for their performance at New Market Heights and Chafin's Farm in September 1864. About two hundred of the medals were presented in May 1865.

buttermilk cavalry: Same as *buttermilk ranger* (q.v.).

buttermilk ranger: A Southern cavalryman. A derogatory term applied by Southern infantrymen, who regarded cavalrymen (often ordered to the rear during a battle) as soft, even cowardly. *Buttermilk* had long been used to mean worthless (because buttermilk is what is left after the butter has been churned out), as in *buttermilk land* for marsh.

butternut: (1) A Confederate uniform dyed with an extract from the butternut tree. Some poor soldiers, unable to afford the usual Confederate gray, wore homemade uniforms colored with the dye, variously described as tan, brownish gray, and light yellowish brown. (2) A Confederate soldier, at first one wearing the butternut uniform, later any Southern soldier. (3) In some Union areas, such as Missouri, a Rebel sympathizer.

butternut cloth (butternut): Cloth dyed with an extract from the butternut tree. The term became widely used during the Civil War because of its association with Confederate uniforms. Aka *nigger cloth* (q.v.).

butternut guerrilla: A Northern scout who wore a Confederate uniform to infiltrate Southern lines.

buzzard's roost: A high-perched signal station, such as one atop a tall tree.

C

C: An abbreviation for *coward* (or *cowardice*). The letter was stamped with indelible ink, or burned with a red-hot iron, onto the hip, hand, cheek, or forehead of an offender.

cacolet: Same as mule *litter* (q.v.).

caisson: A chest for holding, or a usually two-wheeled vehicle for carrying, ammunition. Borrowed from French *caisson* ("large chest"), the word had been used in English since at least the early 1700s.

camp canard: A false report widely believed among the soldiers in a camp.

camp chest: Among Confederate soldiers early in the war, a chest filled with food and kitchenware for use by a small group of men. The cumbersome chests were soon discarded, and bulky food-related items were later handled by quartermasters and commissaries.

camp fever: Typhoid, frequently contracted by soldiers in camp. The term had been in use since the colonial period.

camp itch: A minor but irritating skin disease common among soldiers in camp.

camp kettle: An artillery missile.

camp kit: A compact box that held a soldier's cooking and eating utensils. Patented in 1864.

Canaan (Happy Land of Canaan): The place where Yankees aimed to send the Rebels—the hereafter. The hymn "The Happy Land of Canaan" was a popular Union marching song, and the Northern soldiers' version stressed "sending Rebels to the Happy Land of Canaan."

candlestick: A soldiers' derisive term for the bayonet, which, though seldom used as a weapon, could be thrust into the ground so that its upturned socket would hold a candle. Sometimes other items were used as, and called, candlesticks, such as potatoes. See also *tent peg*.

canned: Preserved in a sealed can. The canned-food industry began shortly before the Civil War, but it was the wartime production of canned products, especially the canned rations given to the soldiers, that made most Americans aware of such food. *Canned vegetables, canned tomatoes, canned goods,* and *canned milk* were familiar expressions of the period.

canned hellfire: Canister.

cannon fever: A violent aversion to combat. A soldier so diagnosed was often transferred to a rear-area assignment.

carpet knight: (1) In the North, a member of the National Guard. The term had been used since at least the 1500s in England for a stay-at-home soldier, or one used to luxury. (2) In the South, a name given by Confederate soldiers to any member of John Mosby's partisan rangers. Aka *feather-bed soldier* and *spoiled darling*.

carte de visite: A portrait photograph on a small card, typically 2¼" by 3¾". The French phrase means "visiting card," so called because of the card's original purpose in Europe in the 1850s. In America, millions of cartes de visite were produced during the Civil War as mementos that soldiers exchanged with their families.

cartridge class: A group, often a ladies' organization, engaged in making cartridges for soldiers.

cashier, to: To dismiss from the service, especially dishonorably. The expression had been in use in English since the sixteenth century, when it was borrowed from Dutch *casseren*, having the same meaning, during a British campaign in the Netherlands.

casket: A coffin. This use of the word came into fashion during the Civil War. Previously it had designated a small box for jewels.

change base, to: To retreat or decamp. The phrase was often used satirically after General McClellan coined it as a euphemistic reference to his defeat in the Peninsula campaign against Richmond in 1862: "Never did such a change of base, involving a retrograde movement, and under incessant attacks...partake of so little disorder."

change one's breath, to: To have a drink of liquor.

cheesebox (cheesebox on a raft, cheesebox upon a plank, Yankee cheesebox on a raft, etc.): A Confederate term of derision for the U.S.S. *Monitor* and any similarly built Union ship, i.e., one with a low, flat deck (the "raft") and at least one revolving turret (the "cheesebox"). Aka *tin can on a shingle*.

cheese knife: A sword or saber.

cheval-de-frise (plural, chevaux-de-frise): A log with sharp, projecting spikes, often used as a defense against cavalry charges. The expression, French for "horse from Friesland" (so called because the log "horse" was first employed by the Frisians), had been an English military term since the seventeenth century.

chicken guts: A slang term for the elaborate cuff braiding that indicated rank on the uniforms of Confederate officers.

children by brevet: Illegitimate children. See also *brevet*.

chin music: (1) Light conversation. A slang expression in use since at least the 1830s. (2) A playful "music" made with the teeth (sounding like rattling bones), played by striking the chin with the hands.

Choctaw: In Georgia, in the period just before the war, a member of a secret society sworn to secession. The group took its name from a Southern tribe of Indians.

Christian Commission (United States Christian Commission): An organization that worked with the United States Sanitary Commission for the relief of soldiers at the front. Founded by the YMCA in New York City in 1861.

city class: See *Pook turtles*.

city delivery service: See *free city delivery*.

Civil War: The military conflict between the Union (North) and the Confederacy (South), 1861-65. This name was recorded early in the war, and though many other names were used both during and after the hostilities, *Civil War* has become the standard term.

Coal and Iron Police: Private police forces hired by Northern industrialists to suppress coal-field draft riots late in the Civil War.

coal torpedo: An explosive device that was machined to look like a lump of coal, blackened, and placed into an enemy coal bin so that it would be shoveled into a furnace, where it would explode. See also *torpedo*.

cockade: See *blue cockade*.

coercionist: One who favored using coercive measures to force the Southern states to remain in the Union.

coffee boiler: A straggler. So named because after such a man lagged behind to avoid a march or a battle or to be intentionally captured (so that he could spend the rest of the war in the "safety" of a prison camp), he often claimed that he had simply stopped to boil a cup of coffee.

coffee cooler: A skulker. So named because he spent so much of his time bending over coffee instead of doing his share of the work or fighting. (In the post-Civil War army, the term came to be applied specifically to a soldier who had a soft office job, one who had plenty of time to drink his coffee leisurely.)

coffee-mill gun: See *Ager gun*.

color: (1) A unit flag flown by foot soldiers. The term had long been used for various flags in England and America. Cf. *ensign* (1) and *standard*. (2) (often capital C and plural) The national flag. Cf. *ensign* (1).

color-bearer: A soldier who carried a *color* (q.v [1] and [2]). The term originated near the beginning of the Civil War. Cf. *standard-bearer*.

color guard: A small group of soldiers serving as guards of honor accompanying a flag.

color line: A line of stacked rifles at which the colors rested.

comin' with a bone in her teeth: An expression often used to describe a vessel moving briskly through water, with white foam at the prow.

commissary: A kind of whiskey issued by the army's commissary department.

committee of safety: Early in the war, a term applied to any of various home-guard organizations in the South.

Committee of Thirteen: A group of thirteen legislators appointed by the United States Senate in late 1860 to investigate measures to avert the disunion crisis.

Committee of Thirty-three: The United States House of Representatives' counterpart to the Senate's Committee of Thirteen.

Committee on the Conduct of the War (in full, Joint Committee on the Conduct of the War): A committee consisting of members of both houses of the United States Congress and providing a civilian investigation of the Union war effort. It was established in late 1861, was dominated by Radical Republicans, and lasted till 1865.

commodore: The naval equivalent of brigadier general, above a captain and below a rear admiral. Used in England since the seventeenth century, but not in America till the United States Congress officially created the rank in 1862. Unofficially, the title had long been applied to the commander of a squadron. See also *admiral*.

company bean boiler: A company cook.

company fund: A fund accumulated by various means and meant to be used by a company commander to buy supplementary food and other supplies for his men. Such funds had been in the army since at least the early nineteenth century.

Company Q: (1) The sick list, especially as occupied by malingerers. (2) A group of Confederate cavalrymen who had lost their horses and were unable to replace them. (3) A company of Union officers reduced to the ranks because of cowardice but given a chance to redeem themselves. All three of these senses probably developed from *quod*, an old slang word (originally in the British underworld) for prison.

Comrades of the Southern Cross: A fraternal organization among Confederate army soldiers, founded in 1863 by Confederate Major General Patrick R. Cleburne and others.

concentrated milk: Another name for *condensed milk* (q.v.).

condensed corn: Hard liquor.

condensed milk: Milk evaporated and sweetened to preserve it. Patented in 1856 by Gail Borden, it first became widely known when it was ordered as a field ration for Union troops.

Confed: (1) A Confederate, i.e., a citizen of the Southern Confederacy or a member of its armed forces. (2) Confederate paper currency or a single bill of such money. See also *blueback*, *grayback* (2), and *shucks*. Cf. *greenback*.

Confederacy: The Confederate States of America. The word had earlier been used to designate the American states under the Articles of Confederation and, later, the United States as a political unit. As early as 1829, *Confederacy* was being applied to the Southern states as a unit.

Confederate: (1) (noun) A citizen or soldier of the Southern Confederacy. In plural, the Confederacy or its military forces. (2) (adjective) Pertaining to the Southern Confederacy. The word appeared in many combinations, such as *Confederate Congress*, *Confederate money*, and *Confederate vessel*. Distinctive examples follow.

Confederate army: An informal name for either the *Army of the Confederate States of America* (q.v.) or the *Provisional Army of the Confederate States* (q.v.).

Confederate Bars: Same as *The Bars* (q.v.).

Confederate Battle Flag: See *Battle Flag, Confederate*.

Confederate beef: (1) Southern cows and horses. A term applied by Union troops to the animals that they killed and ate. (2) Mule meat. A facetious designation used by Confederate soldiers after Grant's 1863 siege of Vicksburg had forced them to resort to eating mules.

Confederate candle: A substitute candle made of beeswax and rosin.

Confederate coffee: Any of various substitutes for coffee beans, such as rye, chicory, or sweet potatoes.

Confederate cotton: Same as *blockade cotton* (q.v.).

Confederate cruiser: Any of the naval ships built by England and France for the South early in the war.

Confederated States: The Confederate States of America. Before the Civil War, the term had been used in reference to the states of the United States in allusion to the theory of state sovereignty under the Constitution.

Confederate duck: Beefsteak around a stuffing of stale bread crumbs.

Confederate flag: A popular name for the *Stars and Bars* (q.v.).

Confederate gray: The gray uniform worn by Confederate soldiers.

Confederate grayback: A legal-tender note of the Confederate government. Aka *grayback*.

Confederate National Flag: See *National Flag, Confederate*.

Confederate Naval Jack: See *Naval Jack, Confederate*.

Confederate needle: A needle made from a hawthorn bush.

Confederate note: Same as *Confederate scrip* (q.v.).

Confederate paper: A coarse, yellow, homemade paper.

Confederate ram: A Confederate warship fitted with an iron beak on the bow.

Confederate scrip: Paper currency issued by the Confederate government. Aka *Confederate note*.

Confederate secret weapon: A nickname for the *Williams rapid-fire gun* (q.v.).

Confederate stamp: A postage stamp issued by the Confederate government.

Confederate States (Confederate States of America): The states composing the Southern Confederacy.

Confederate States Army: Same as *Army of the Confederate States of America* (q.v.).

Confederate States Army Signal Corps: See *Signal Corps*.

Confederate States Regular Army: See *Army of the Confederate States of America*.

Confederate syrup: Sorghum syrup, which was widely produced in the South.

confederationist: A supporter of the Confederate States of America.

confiscate, to: To steal, especially from civilians. A soldiers' euphemistic term borrowed from governmental usage of the same verb, which officially meant to seize the property of enemies under certain legal conditions.

confiscation: A government's seizure of property belonging to opposing civilian and military populations. Both sides established laws providing for confiscation.

The word *confiscation*, in this sense, had been in use since the sixteenth century.

Congressional Medal of Honor: Same as *Medal of Honor* (q.v.).

conscription: The compulsory enrollment of men for military service. Both sides had to resort to conscription, beginning in 1862. The word *conscription*, in this sense, had been in use since the turn of the nineteenth century. See also *draft*.

consecrated milk: A soldiers' humorous misnomer for *concentrated milk* (q.v.).

Conserve Slavery party: A Northern political party favoring the continuance of slavery, active in 1862.

consolidated milk: Another name for *condensed milk* (q.v.).

Constitutional Union party: A party of Southern Whigs and others who ignored the slavery issue and favored the continuance of the Union. The name had also been used in 1850 by Georgians opposed to disunion.

Constitution as it is, the, the Union as it was: A Democratic campaign slogan created in 1862 by the Ohio politician Clement Laird Vallandigham.

Conthieveracy: The Southern Confederacy. An abusive name inspired by the South's seizure of United States property at the outset of the Civil War.

contraband (contraband of war): A slave who sought protection by, or was confiscated by, the Union. Benjamin F. Butler originated this sense of the term in 1861. Newspapers sometimes used the expression *intelligent contraband*. *Contraband* had meant smuggling or smuggled goods since the sixteenth century, and, since the eighteenth century, anything (such as arms) forbidden to be supplied to one belligerent in a war and subject to being seized by the other.

cook stove: An artillery missile. Soldiers' slang.

coosh: See *cush*.

copperbottom: A Missourian who sympathized with the South. The copperbottom is a red-bellied water snake. Cf. *copperhead*.

copperhead: (1) A Northerner who sympathized with the South, especially a Northern Democrat who opposed Lincoln and his war policy. The word had previously designated a venomous snake (since at least 1775), a disliked person or group (since the early 1800s), and a Democratic faction in Pennsylvania (in the 1840s). (2) A badge (typically a copper coin with an Indian head on one side) worn by a copperhead. *Copperhead* was applied to a person by at least July 1861; the badges were not used till 1862.

copperheadism: The beliefs and practices of a *copperhead* (q.v.).

coppery: Sympathetic to copperheads.

Corn-fed-racy: A Union soldiers' name for the Confederacy, derived from the large role of corn in the Southern diet.

corduroy (corduroy road): A road made of logs laid side by side transversely. Often used during the war to cross muddy or swampy areas. The name was established by the early 1800s and was borrowed from that of a heavy ribbed cloth. The word was frequently used as a verb or verbal (such as *corduroying* as a noun). A *corduroy bridge* was constructed along the same lines.

corn wine: Hard liquor of poor quality. A Southern term.

corps badge: An ornament on a soldier's uniform or hat to identify his corps. Before the Civil War, badges were not generally used beyond the regimental level. Corps badges were popularized by the *Kearny patch* (q.v.).

cotton blockade: The Federal blockade of Southern ports to prevent the shipping of cotton abroad.

cotton clad: A vessel protected, or "armored," with cotton bales. The term was often used as an adjective, as in "cotton-clad steamboats." Cf. *cotton gunboat* (1).

cotton Confederacy: The Southern Confederacy.

Cottondom: The Southern states. The term originated before the war. Aka *Cottonia*.

cotton famine: The lack of cotton in England caused by the Union's blockade of Southern ports.

cotton gunboat: (1) A river boat armored with cotton bales and used by the Confederates in the defense of New Orleans. Cf. *cotton clad*. (2) A Southern gunboat used to run the cotton blockade.

Cottonia: The Southern states. A term less frequently found than its synonym *Cottondom*.

cotton Rebel: A Southerner during the Civil War.

coup de main: A sudden attack in force, usually to capture a position quickly. The expression, French for "stroke of hand," had been in use in English since at least the mid-1700s.

covered-bridge gun: Same as *Requa battery* (q.v.).

cracker line: A transportation line for food supplies. The term is particularly associated with the Union steamboat line opened on the Tennessee River in 1863 to replace the railroad route to Chattanooga that had been cut off by the Confederates.

creeper: A type of frying pan used by Union troops early in the war. Soon the pan was discarded and men fried food in a tin plate or in half a canteen.

crimp: A *bounty broker* (q.v.) who consistently supplied recruits of low character or with physical disabilities. Aka *runner* (1). Since the mid-1700s, the term *crimp* had been used in England for an agent who procured seamen and soldiers by entrapping or impressing them.

Crittenden Compromise: A December 1860 proposal by Senator John J. Crittenden of Kentucky to end the conflict between North and South peacefully. In July 1861 he also put forward the *Crittenden Resolution* with a similar purpose.

critter company: A cavalry company.

crooked shoe: Either of a pair of shoes cut in the modern fashion, for left and right feet. Before the Civil War, the simpler, cheaper straight shoes, which could fit either foot, were most common. Crooked shoes were issued as part of the Civil War uniform.

crow's-foot (crowfoot): A device with four metal points arranged so that three points would be on the ground and one would stick up as a defense against cavalry. So named because it resembled a crow's foot. The term had been in use since the eighteenth century, and an older word for the same weapon, *caltrop*, went back to at least the sixteenth century.

crumb: A body louse, because of its small size.

C.S. (C.S.A.): Abbreviation for the Confederate States of America.

cush (coosh): Any of a variety of Southern dishes made with cornmeal or crumbled cornbread. Typically a soldier would fry the cornmeal in bacon grease, or stew it with bacon grease, beef, and water. *Cush* is of African origin and ultimately goes back to an Arabic word meaning "couscous." Aka *sloosh* or *slosh*. Sometimes the cornmeal was swirled in bacon grease and then wrapped around a ramrod for cooking over an open fire; this form of the dish was also called *ramrod bread* (q.v.).

D

D: An abbreviation for *deserter* (or *desertion*). The letter was stamped with indelible ink, or burned with a red-hot iron, onto the hip, hand, cheek, or forehead of an offender.

Dahlgren (Dahlgren gun): A standard Union navy artillery smoothbore, designed by John A.B. Dahlgren and officially adopted in 1856. Because of its shape, it was nicknamed the *soda-pop gun* and *soda-water bottle*. Several other weapons of the 1840s and 1850s were known as Dahlgrens.

Dahlgren papers: Documents found on the body of the Union colonel Ulric Dahlgren after he was killed on March 2, 1864, near Richmond, Virginia. The papers contained plans to burn Richmond and murder Jefferson Davis and his cabinet.

dandyfunk: A navy stew of hardtack soaked in water and baked with salt pork and molasses.

David: A Federal term for any Confederate torpedo boat patterned after the C.S.S. *David*, i.e., a cigar-shaped, semisubmersible steamer armed with a spar torpedo.

The name referred to the biblical slayer of the giant (the Union).

Davis boot: A type of shoe that rose to just above the ankle and was tied in front with a lace. A few standard sizes fit most men. It was named for Jefferson Davis, who was secretary of war when the shoe was developed. During the Civil War, both Union and Confederate soldiers wore the Jefferson boot.

Davisdom: The Confederate States of America. So nicknamed after its president, Jefferson Davis.

Davis Guard Medal: A medal presented by the residents of Sabine City, Texas, to the Davis Guards after their victory at Sabine Pass, Texas, in 1863.

deadbeat: Same as *beat* (q.v.).

dead cart: A soldiers' term for an ambulance. Since the early 1700s, the same expression had designated a cart that actually carried dead bodies.

deadhead: A noncombatant accompanying a fighting force.

deadline: At a prison, the line beyond which guards would shoot a prisoner dead.

dead rope: A rope marking the *deadline* (q.v.).

dead shot: Another name for *forty-rod* (q.v.), because it could place a deadly shot at forty rods.

death bells: A soldiers' term for hardtack.

defeat in detail, to: See *in detail*.

demand note: A note redeemable on demand, issued by the Federal government as currency.

Democratico-Slavic: A term designating the Democratic party and suggesting its proslavery attitude.

desecrated vegetables: A soldiers' sarcastic term for *desiccated vegetables* (q.v.).

deserter: See *galvanized*.

desiccated potatoes: Dried potato slabs issued to Union troops. Aka *pulverized potatoes*.

desiccated vegetables: Dehydrated mixed vegetables issued in solid form to Federal soldiers.

detached volunteers: Infantrymen who were detached from their regiments for temporary service in the artillery.

devil fish: A Federal term for a fish-shaped Confederate torpedo. Several of the torpedoes were fastened together by wire so that when struck by the bow of a vessel, fuses would ignite.

Dictator: A nickname for the heavy thirteen-inch seacoast mortar mounted on a railroad flatcar and used by the

Federals in the siege of Petersburg, Virginia, in 1864. Aka *Petersburg Express*.

discharge: A wound that was not life-threatening but was serious enough to lead to a permanent release from the service.

disloyalist: Someone not loyal to the Union.

District Emancipation Act: An act freeing District of Columbia slaves and reimbursing their owners, passed by both houses of Congress and signed by President Lincoln in 1862.

ditch: The Confederate soldiers' usual term for a military trench.

ditch hunter: A Northern term for a Southern soldier. The expression originated after a few retreats by Confederates early in the war, Rebel leaders having vowed to fight "to the last ditch." See also *Ditchland*.

Ditchland: A Northern term for the Southern Confederacy, whose leaders had vowed to fight "to the last ditch." See also *ditch hunter*.

Dixie: The South. The term was popularized through the song "Dixie's Land" (1859), by Daniel Decatur Emmett, a Northern entertainer. Many farfetched theories have been proposed for the origin of the word *Dixie*. But the earliest known record of the word is in the 1850 play *The United States Mail and Dixie in Difficulty*, in which the main black character is named Dixie. Dixie, in fact, was a common name for black characters in minstrel shows, and Emmett himself stated that he and other Northern showmen routinely used the term *Dixie's land* to mean the "black (slave)'s land," i.e., the South.

dog collar: A stiff leather cravat fastened around the neck with a buckle. Prescribed by Federal army regulations but rarely worn.

doghouse: Another name for a *dog tent* (q.v.). Aka *pup tent, shelter tent,* and *tente d'abri* (q.v. all).

dog robber: A Northern soldiers' term for a cook.

dogsbody: A sailors' term for dried peas boiled in a cloth. The expression had been used since at least the early 1800s.

dog tent: An informal name for the *shelter tent* (q.v.). So called because it was so small that it looked like a dog's house. Aka *doghouse, pup tent,* and *tente d'abri* (q.v. all).

Doodle: A Union soldier. Short for *Yankee Doodle.*

double ender: A gunboat with both ends similarly rounded.

double note: A piece of paper money with different issues printed on the two sides. Common in the South because of the paper shortage.

doughboy: A United States Army infantryman. The term is most closely associated with World War I, but it evolved during, or just before, the Civil War. Of the several theories about the origin of the term, two are widely accepted: an infantryman was a doughboy because (1) he wore a uniform with large globular brass buttons (a globular dumpling had long been known as a doughboy), or (2) he cleaned his white belt with "dough" made of pipe clay.

doughface: A Northerner who favored the South in the Civil War. Before the war, the same term had designated a Northern congressman who did not oppose slavery and its extension. The word implied that the person was made of dough, i.e., he was easily molded by others. Earlier, by at least 1809, *doughface* had meant a mask literally made of dough.

down the line: See *go down the line, to.*

draft: A method of selecting men for compulsory military service. The Confederacy established a draft in 1862. The Union instituted a limited draft through militias in the same year, but finally moved to a full national draft in 1863. The word *draft* had been used with this meaning since the eighteenth century.

draftee: A person drafted for military service.

draft riot: Any one of many Northern riots against the Federal draft. The worst riots occurred in New York City in July 1863.

drawn over the left, to be: To be drafted. *Over the left* was an early Victorian catchphrase expressing a negative (*left* being unlucky, as in "left-handed compliment"). One specific sense of *over the left* was "in the wrong way," and when a man's name was drawn for the draft, it was, for him, drawn the wrong way, i.e, over the left.

draw over the left, to: To steal. Here, *to draw* was used in the same sense as it was in the military phrase "to draw rations." *Over the left* meant "in the wrong way." See also *drawn over the left, to be.*

duff: A boiled pudding of flour and water, often sweetened with molasses and dried fruit. Chiefly a navy dish. *Duff*, an English dialectal variant of *dough*, had been used with this meaning since at least the 1830s.

Dutch: A Southern term for a Yankee, especially a Northern sympathizer in Missouri. The word had, of course, long been used for an immigrant from the Netherlands or from Germany (Deutschland), and by the mid-1800s a *Dutchman* was any foreigner. After secession, a Yankee was a foreigner to a Rebel.

E

Eads ironclads: Same as *Pook turtles* (q.v.).

easier to carry extra bullets than a stretcher: A popular saying during the Civil War, a response to those military leaders who balked at the use of repeating weapons because of the possibility of wasting ammunition.

eat the dishrag, to: To eat a piece of bread that had been used to clean a plate.

echelon: A formation of successive parallel units of troops with each unit somewhat to the left or right of the one in the rear, like a series of steps. Often found in the prepositional phrase *in echelon* (or French *en échelon*). The word was borrowed from French, where the original meaning was "rung of a ladder." In English since the late 1700s.

Egypt of the West: Abraham Lincoln's term for the interior region of the United States, between the Alleghenies and the Rocky Mountains.

eight-day man: A contemptuous term for someone who joined the army for only a brief period.

Emancipation Act: Same as *Emancipation Proclamation* (q.v.).

Emancipation Amendment: Same as *Emancipation Proclamation* (q.v.).

Emancipation Message: Same as *Emancipation Proclamation* (q.v.).

Emancipation Proclamation: President Lincoln's proclamation freeing all slaves in those areas in rebellion against the United States. It was announced in September 1862 through the *preliminary Emancipation Proclamation* (q.v.) and took effect on January 1, 1863.

emancipationist: Anyone in sympathy with President Lincoln's *Emancipation Proclamation* (q.v.).

embalmed beef: Soldiers' slang for canned meat.

encased postage stamp: A postage stamp (of varying denomination) encased by a circular brass frame with a clear frontpiece so that the stamp could be seen. John Gault created this product in 1862 and sold it in quantity to Northern merchants, who used it as *stamp money* (q.v.) to give change to customers, coins having become scarce during the war.

en échelon: See *echelon*.

Enfield rifle (Enfield rifle-musket): One of the standard shoulder firearms on both sides of the Civil War. It was named after the English town where a small-arms factory produced the original weapon adopted by the British army in the mid-1850s.

enfilade: Gunfire that sweeps the entire length of an enemy battle line, or a position favorable for such firing. The word entered the English language by the early 1700s from French, where it was based on a verb meaning "to thread on a string," hence "to pierce or traverse from end to end."

ensign: (1) A national flag flown on a ship. The term, borrowed from Middle French and based on a Latin word for "insignia," had long been used for various flags in England and America. Cf. *color* (1) and (2) and *standard*. (2) The lowest commissioned rank in the United States Navy. It was officially adopted in 1862, replacing the title *passed midshipman*.

Ericsson's Folly: An early derisive nickname for John Ericsson's *Monitor*, the first Union ironclad.

Erlanger loan: A transaction in which Emile Erlanger and Company, a Parisian banking firm, managed the sale of a large Confederate bond issue secured by cotton.

essence of coffee: An extract of coffee mixed with sugar and milk, a kind of Civil War version of instant coffee. It was issued in the field to Northern soldiers, who hated it. The pasty stuff was soon discontinued. Aka *extract of coffee*.

ethnogenesis: The formation or emergence of a group within a larger community. In his "Ethnogenesis" (1861), the Southern poet Henry Timrod praised the birth of the Confederacy. *Ethnogenesis* combines *ethno-* ("race, people") and genesis ("the origin, coming into being").

European brigade: An armed body of men organized among non-English-speaking residents of New Orleans during the Civil War. Aka *European legion* and *foreign legion*.

European legion: Same as *European brigade* (q.v.).

European stovepipe: Any one of the poor-quality shoulder firearms purchased from Europe by the North and the South early in the war.

evacuation of Corinth: Name given to diarrhea or dysentery among the Confederate soldiers at Corinth, Mississippi, just prior to the Battle of Shiloh in 1862.

Excelsior hand grenade: A hand grenade with an outer shell in two parts that could easily break apart. So dangerous to handle that only a few were made. Patented by W.W. Hanes in 1862.

Excelsior hat: A Southern name for the *Whipple hat* (q.v.).

execute a flank movement, to: To evade lice by turning underwear inside out. *Flank* here means "escape." See also *flank, to*.

explosive bullet: Same as *musket shell* (q.v.).

extract of coffee: Same as *essence of coffee* (q.v.).

F

faith paper: Paper currency not redeemable in gold or silver. A sarcastic term used by people used to hard money.

falling collar: A collar that turned down and lay flat on the neck. This term was rare, but it was used in the 1861 *Army Regulations*.

fancy lady: A city prostitute in an elegant brothel. Aka *boarder*.

fascine: A long bundle of wooden sticks tied together and used for such purposes as filling ditches and raising batteries. *Fascine* was borrowed in the seventeenth century from a French word, which in turn was based on Latin for "a bundle."

fascine knife: A type of sawtooth bayonet developed in 1864.

Fast-Footed Virginians: A Union soldiers' interpretation of *F.F.V.*, originally meaning "First Families of Virginia." The Northerners were goading the Virginians as ones who fled from battle. See also *Flat-Footed Virginians*.

fast trick: A woman with a loose reputation. Cf. *pretty rapid little case*.

feather-bed soldier: Same as *carpet knight* (2) (q.v.). The expression had been used since at least the 1830s for a soldier who had an easy job.

Fed: Short for *Federal* (q.v.). During the revolutionary war, a Fed was a member of the Federal party.

Federal: A Northerner or a Union soldier. In plural, the North or its army. During the American Revolution, a Federal was a member of the Federal party.

Federal army: The Union army. The same term applied to the pre-Civil War United States Army.

Federal blue: The blue cloth of the army uniform worn by Federal troops, or the uniform itself.

Federalist: A Union soldier. During the American Revolution, a member of the Federal (aka Federalist) party, one who sought the adoption of the Federal Constitution.

Federal officer: An officer in the Federal army. The term had earlier meant any of various officials of the United States government.

ferryboat: A Union soldiers' term for a broad army shoe.

F.F.V.: An abbreviation for *First Families of Virginia*. The abbreviation had been in use since at least the 1840s. Northern soldiers derisively interpreted the abbreviation as *Fast-Footed Virginians* (q.v.) and *Flat-Footed Virginians* (q.v.).

Fifteen-Negro Law (Fifteen-Nigger Law, Fifteen-Slave Law) *See Twenty-Negro Law.*

fifth wheel: An early derisive nickname for the *Sanitary Commission* (q.v.), based on the belief that the organization might interfere with the government's treatment of soldiers. *Fifth wheel* had long been a proverbial expression designating something superfluous.

fight it out on this line, to: To persevere to the end. The phrase became well known when General Grant used it in an official dispatch after the Battle of Spotsylvania Court House, Virginia, in May 1864: "I propose to fight it out on this line if it takes all summer."

fight the tiger, to: See *tiger.*

fight under the black flag, to: To kill lice. A black flag had long symbolized death or deadly purpose. For example, it was formerly hoisted in prisons as a signal that someone had been executed.

file closer: A soldier who made sure that a formation of troops stayed in order. The term had been in use since at least the early 1800s.

fire and fall back, to: To throw up.

fireball: A hardened lump of sand, wet clay, sawdust, and coal dust. Southern civilians used fireballs to heat their homes when coal became scarce.

fire-eater: A violent, uncompromising Southern partisan. The term had been used with this meaning since at least the 1840s, when fire-eaters were already advocating secession. Since the 1600s, the word *fire-eater* had designated a performer who pretended to eat fire.

Fire Zouave: A member of one of the Union volunteer companies of former New York City firemen who adopted the dress and drill of the Zouaves. See also *Zouave*.

first-call men: Men who responded to the initial plea for Union soldiers and volunteered for three years' service in 1861.

first class: A postal category mainly for letters. United States mail service was divided into classes in 1863. *Second class* covered various printed items, and *third class* included miscellaneous material, such as seeds and garden bulbs.

flag officer: From the late 1850s to 1862, the only official title of a senior naval officer, above the rank of captain. In 1862 the ranks of *commodore* (q.v.) and *rear admiral* (see *admiral*) were created to begin the process of replacing *flag officer*. In the British navy, *flag officer* had long designated a officer entitled to fly a personal flag indicating his rank, i.e., a rear admiral, vice admiral, or full admiral (the modern United States Navy follows a similar practice).

flag raising: The raising, or the ceremony surrounding the raising, of the United States flag. This practice became a rage at both public and private locations during the wave of patriotism in 1861.

flank, to: To evade, deceive, steal, sneak, or escape. Soldiers extended the military sense of this verb, to turn or pass around (an enemy's flank), so that to avoid irksome duty was to flank it; to flank a farmer out of his pig was to take it on the sly; to sneak into a mess line was to flank into it; to slip past a guard for the purpose of deserting or taking an unauthorized leave was to *flank the guard* or *to flank the sentinel*.

flanker: A person who flanked. The word was often applied to a thief, especially a sneaky, as opposed to a brazen, one.

Flat-Footed Virginians: A Union soldiers' insulting interpretation of *F.F.V.*, originally meaning "First Families of Virginia." See also *Fast-Footed Virginians*.

floating battery: A Confederate soldiers' term for army bread. The phrase had also long designated a raft or barge fitted up with weapons and used as a battery.

flying battery: A group of two or more horse-drawn cannons quickly moving through a battlefield and firing from different positions.

Flying Telegraph Train: Two mobile wagons loaded with equipment for the *Beardslee Telegraph* (q.v.) system.

foot cavalry: Stonewall Jackson's infantrymen. So called because of their legendary swiftness afoot.

forage, to: (1) To rove in search of provisions, taken by plundering if necessary. This expression had been in use since at least the fifteenth century. (2) To steal, a Civil War soldiers' slang interpretation of this word.

forage cap: A small military cap with a round flat crown, used for fatigue purposes.

foreign legion: Same as *European brigade* (q.v.).

Fort Pickens Medals: Medals awarded in 1862 by the New York Chamber of Commerce to the Union defenders of Fort Pickens (in Florida) early in the war.

Fort Sumter Medals: Medals awarded in 1862 to the Union defenders of Fort Sumter (in South Carolina) early in the war.

forty acres and a mule: An expression common among blacks near the end of, and just after, the war, stating their belief that confiscated plantations would be divided up and given to freedmen. This misunderstanding may have originated with General Sherman's January 1865 order to divide among freedmen some lands on the southeast coast. Earlier in the war, Union propagandists had started this line of thinking by mentioning *ten acres and a mule*.

forty dead men: The rounds of ammunition in a cartridge box.

forty-rod: Cheap whiskey, so strong it could kill at forty rods.

Forward to Richmond/Washington! **(On to Richmond/Washington!)**: A battle cry demanding an aggressive military policy by, respectively, the North and the South. The expression began with a June 1861 editorial in the *New York Tribune*, "Forward to Richmond!" Other newspapers took up the phrase and shortened it to *On to Richmond!* Soon the South responded with *Forward to Washington!* and *On to Washington!*

fractional currency: A generic term in the North for various kinds of paper money issued in denominations under one dollar: (1) informally for *stamp money* (q.v.); (2) more accurately for *postage currency* (q.v.); (3) officially, beginning with an October 1863 issue, for bills actually labeled *fractional currency*. All of these replaced coins, which became scarce during the war. The South, too, printed many kinds of fractional currency.

fractional note: A piece of *fractional currency* (3) (q.v.) or *postage currency* (q.v.).

free city delivery: Free home delivery of mail in cities. In 1863 the United States government initiated this service, which also spawned the expressions *city delivery service* and *free delivery*.

free delivery: See *free city delivery*.

freedman: A black slave freed by the Civil War.

Freedmen's Bank (Freedmen's Savings and Trust Company): A bank established by the United States Congress in spring 1865 to encourage liberated slaves to save money for land and homes.

Freedmen's Bureau (Bureau of Refugees, Freedmen, and Abandoned Lands): A bureau created by the United States Congress in spring 1865 to oversee welfare programs for liberated slaves.

free fighter: A *partisan ranger* (q.v.) or a *guerrilla* (q.v.).

freight train: An artillery missile.

French leave: An unauthorized furlough. The term was often used in the expressions *to take a French* and *to take French leave*. The expression came from the eighteenth century French custom of going away from a social gathering without bothering to take leave of the host or hostess; *French leave* was recorded in this social sense as early as 1771.

fresh fish: A new recruit in the service or a new prisoner in a prisoner-of-war camp.

Friends Society: Same as *Sons of the South* (1) (q.v.).

G

gabion: A cylindrical basket filled with earth or rocks and used in building fieldworks. The term was borrowed in the sixteenth century from Middle French, which in turn was based on an Old Italian word meaning "large cage."

gallinipper: Any of various insects, especially a large mosquito. The term was recorded by at least the early 1800s.

galvanized: Reactivated as a soldier, after a period as a prisoner of war, by swearing allegiance to, and enlisting in the army of, one's captors. A soldier who went through this metamorphosis was termed a *galvanized Rebel/Confederate* or a *galvanized Yankee*. However, the two terms were never absolutely distinguished during the war, and they have continued to cause confusion in postwar writings. Most modern historians use *galvanized Yankee* to mean a Rebel soldier who joined the Union army, and *galvanized Rebel/Confederate* to mean a Union soldier who joined the Confederate army. However, the opposite definitions sometimes apply. To determine which meanings are intended, the careful reader must examine the context of a given passage. The word *galvanized* may have been selected to mean "recoated" (as in *galvanized iron*), but more likely to mean "reborn," a reference to the mid-nineteenth century experiments in using galvanism (electricity developed by chemical action) to regenerate life in dead tissue. Alternative names for one or the other of the above terms included *deserter*, *Rebel prisoner*, *repentant Rebel*, *transfugee* (q.v.), *U.S. Volunteer*, and *whitewashed Rebel*.

gasoline: A volatile flammable liquid refined from petroleum. During the Civil War, gasoline was in the early stages of its development.

Gatling gun: A light, rapid-fire, multiple-barrel forerunner of the machine gun, powered by a hand crank. It was developed by Richard J. Gatling early in the war and used sparingly by the Union in the late stages of the conflict.

General Bragg's bodyguard: Same as *Bragg's bodyguard* (q.v.).

ghost: A white horse.

gigadier breneral (jigadier brindle): A wordplay on *brigadier general*.

Gillmore Medal (Gillmore Medal of Honor): Bronze medals that the Union commander Quincy A. Gillmore gave to enlisted personnel who had distinguished themselves during operations in South Carolina in 1863.

ginger panada: Same as *panada* (q.v.).

give the vermin a parole, to: To throw away an infested article of clothing.

glacis: A slope running down from the parapet of a covered way and meeting the ground so as to expose attackers to firing from the ramparts. The term had been used since the late 1600s, when it was borrowed from French, the original sense being "slippery place."

glory hole: An outpost between enemy lines. The term had previously been used for a variety of things suggesting discomfort, such as a small compartment on a ship and the mouth of a glassmaking furnace.

gobble (gobble up), to: To steal, defeat, or capture. All of these were extensions of the original meaning of the verb: to eat greedily or swallow hastily.

go down the line, to: To visit a brothel. To be *down the line* was to be in the brothel district.

God's country: A Union troops' term for the North, especially when they were battling not only Rebels but also Southern heat, humidity, and mosquitoes.

God's flag: A Union term for the United States flag.

go in search of his rights, to: To retreat, said of a Rebel by a Yank.

gold certificate: A document certifying that the United States Treasury had deposited gold for redeeming the certificate. Gold certificates were authorized by Congress in 1863.

Golden Circle: Short for *Knights of the Golden Circle* (q.v.).

Gold Hoax: A scheme implemented in 1864 by the journalist Joseph Howard, who, to make a killing on the gold market, anonymously sent to the New York newspapers a bogus proclamation under President Lincoln's name, stating that defeat was imminent and calling for the drafting of 400,000 more men.

gone up: Hopeless, desperate, or finished. During the war, this was a popular phrase to describe either minor personal incidents or major historical events, as in "Richmond...was a gone-up case." The expression came from the farm, where a crop parched by drought was said to be gone up (as in "burned up" or "gone up in smoke").

goober (goober grabber): A soldier from a state where peanuts (goobers) were raised, especially Alabama, Georgia, and North Carolina.

goose question: (1) The slavery issue. The origin of the phrase is obscure, but it evolved during the extension-of-slavery debates of the 1840s and 1850s, especially in the Kansas and Nebraska territories. The term was usually shortened to *goose* and embedded in one of the following expressions: *to be all right on the goose, to be right on the goose*, or *to be sound on the goose*. All meant to be orthodox on the slavery issue, i.e., to be proslavery.

gopher: A playful nickname soldiers gave each other because each man spent so much of his time digging, or huddled up in, *a gopher hole* (q.v.).

gopher hole: A shelter that a soldier dug out of the earth when tents and logs were not available.

go South, to: To give up Northern connections and join the Southern Confederacy. In 1861 many United States military leaders resigned and went South.

government on wheels: Jefferson Davis's term for the group of high-level Confederate officials who fled by train from Richmond to Danville, Virginia, late in the war.

grab a root, to: To eat.

grape: (1) A rumor or report obtained by a *grapevine telegraph* (q.v.). (2) Same as *grapevine telegraph* (q.v.).

grapevine: (1) A rumor or report obtained by a *grapevine telegraph* (q.v.). (2) Same as *grapevine telegraph* (q.v.).

grapevine telegraph: Any informal or secret means of conveying information, such as casually between soldiers in different army units or slyly between prisoners of war. The term was allegedly first used in 1859 for a telegraph set up in the Far West to relay news about the Comstock Lode. During the Civil War, the expression may have been prompted by the use of secret telegraph lines that resembled grapevines. However, the common soldier undoubtedly used the term with the idea that the grapevine was his humble substitute for a real telegraph line.

gravel: Same as *night blindness* (q.v.). *Gravel* was short for *gravel-blind* ("nearly stone-blind"), a word that Shakespeare coined as a humorous intensive of *sand-blind*.

gray: (1) The official gray uniform of the Confederate army. (2) A Confederate soldier. The word is often capitalized. (3) The South or its army. Commonly "the Gray."

grayback: (1) A Confederate soldier, whose official uniform was gray. (2) A piece of Confederate paper currency. Confederate bills varied in color depending on place and date of issue. Generically, however, they were called graybacks as a linguistic parallel to Northern greenbacks (paper money), gray being selected, of course, because of its association with the South (as in the army uniform). See also *blueback*, *Confed* (2), and *shucks*. Cf. *greenback*. (3) A body louse.

graycoat: A Confederate soldier, who initially wore a long double-breasted gray tailcoat. Cf. *gray jacket*.

gray jacket: A Confederate soldier. So named by Northerners because of his short-waisted, single-breasted gray jacket, which replaced the traditional military tailcoat. Cf. *graycoat*. (2) A body louse. A sense coined by Northerners but proudly adopted by Rebels as well.

greenback: A legal-tender note used as currency in place of gold, first authorized by the United States government during the Civil War. One side of each bill was printed in green ink. Aka *Treasury greenback*.

greyhound: A Union soldiers' term for a member of any of the fast-moving Confederate infantry regiments from Texas.

greyhounds to march and stayers in a fight: A good infantry regiment.

guard line: The limits of a prison camp.

guerrilla: (1) Someone engaged in irregular warfare, usually a member of an independent unit characterized by its predatory, often lawless, excursions. The term was borrowed in the early 1800s from Spanish, where it is a diminutive of *guerra* ("war"). (2) In some Union areas, notably Illinois, a term for a Rebel sympathizer.

guerrillero: A Southwestern term for a guerrilla. Borrowed from Spanish.

guide center/left/right: (1) Commands to regulate the alignment of a marching unit. (2) Oral directions slyly passed down a line of marching troops, letting the rear soldiers know where to look to see a pretty girl.

guidon: A small pennantlike flag used as a unit marker or as a guide in making and keeping formations. The term was usually associated with cavalry units. The word, borrowed in the sixteenth century from Middle French and meaning "guide," had designated various flags in England before the United States adopted the term by at least the 1840s.

Gulf Confederacy: A confederacy of those states adjacent to the Gulf of Mexico.

Gulf fleet: That part of the Federal fleet operating in the Gulf of Mexico.

gum blanket: A soldiers' name for a blanket, usually in poncho form, made waterproof by being treated with rubber.

gum coat: A coat made of rubber, worn over a soldier's uniform.

gunboat: A slang term for a broad, clumsy army shoe. It reminded soldiers of the awkward-looking gunboats of the time.

gunboat fair: See *ladies' gunboat society*.

gun howitzer: Same as *Napoleon gun* (q.v.).

H

half-shelter: Same as *shelter half* (q.v.).

handcuffed volunteer: A derisive term for any one of the low-quality Union replacements late in the war, largely substitutes and bounty jumpers, often brought up under guard.

Hanes hand grenade: A hand grenade detonated when impact forced one of its interior percussion caps against its outer shell.

Happy Land of Canaan: Same as *Canaan* (q.v.).

hard bread: *Hardtack* (q.v.).

hard cracker: *Hardtack* (q.v.).

hardware: Weapons, especially small arms. This sense of the word seems to have originated during the Civil War. Since the 1500s the word had meant small ware (goods) made of metal.

Hardee hat: The 1858 black-pattern army full-dress head-gear, with a tall, round crown and a wide brim that was usually rolled up on the right side and fastened with a brass eagle, while the left side was decorated with a black plume. The hat was worn early in the Civil War. The style originated in 1855 as a cavalry hat, and in 1858 it was finally adopted for the full army. The hat was named after Major William J. Hardee, a cavalry officer who was on the 1855 board that reviewed the pattern. Aka *Jeff Davis hat* because Jefferson Davis was secretary of war during the mid-1850s, when the hat was being developed.

hardtack: A hard biscuit or cracker of plain flour and water. Its typical size was about three inches square and half an inch thick. The term had been in use since at least the early 1800s. *Tack* was an old word for "food."

hardtack pudding: A dish usually made by pulverizing hardtack, adding water to make a dough, covering it with dried fruit, wrapping it in cloth, and boiling it.

havelock: A cap cover, usually of white cloth, with a long flap in the back to protect the neck from the sun. It was issued early in the war, but it had a short life in the field. This cap cape was named after Henry Havelock, a British general during the Indian Mutiny of 1857.

haversack: A bag similar to a knapsack but strapped over the right shoulder and rested on the left hip. It usually held rations and personal items. *Haversack*, borrowed from French in the eighteenth century, is based on a German word meaning "bag for oats."

hayfoot, strawfoot: A command allegedly used by drill sergeants to teach rustic recruits the difference between the left foot (with hay attached) and the right foot (with straw attached). The expression was recorded by at least the early 1850s. *Hayfoot* and *strawfoot* were also used separately to designate the recruit himself.

headquarters in the saddle: A catchphrase created when Major General John Pope took command of the Union's Army of Virginia in 1862 and he said his headquarters would be "in the saddle." Some observers quipped that he had his headquarters where his hindquarters should be.

hellfire: Cheap, fiery whiskey.

hellfire stew (hell-fired stew): (1) A blend of everything available and eatable (and sometimes uneatable). Aka *hish and hash* (1) and *son of a seadog* (1). (2) Hardtack pulverized, soaked in water, and fried in pork fat. Aka *hish and hash* (2) and *skillygalee* (1).

hellhound: A Confederate term for a Northern gunboat.

Henry (Henry rifle, Henry repeating rifle): A magazine breechloading lever-action shoulder arm invented by Benjamin Tyler Henry just before the war and used in quantity by the Union.

Here's your mule: A nonsense-slang expression used by Union troops to mean "We've been here."

Heroes of America, Order of the: One of three principal Southern groups opposed to secession. Aka *Red-String*

Band and *Red Strings* because members identified themselves by wearing red string on their lapels. See also *Peace and Constitutional Society* and *Peace Society*.

Hessian: A Southern term of derision for a loyalist, especially a Federal soldier. During the Revolutionary War, the British had hired Hessians (German mercenaries, often from Hesse) to fight the Americans.

high private: A facetious term for a mere private, especially one who thought too highly of himself.

high tone: A contemptuous Northern, especially Western, term for a Southern white as representing chivalrous blue bloods from England. In adjective form as *high-toned*, which, since the early 1800s, had been used more broadly to mean pretentious.

hish and hash: (1) A meal of anything available. Aka *hellfire stew* (1) and *son of a seadog* (1). (2) Hardtack pulverized, soaked in water, and fried in pork fat. Aka *hellfire stew* (2) and *skillygalee* (1).

Holy Joe (Holy John): A chaplain.

homegrown Yankee (homemade Yankee): A Rebel term of contempt for a Southerner who sympathized with, or enlisted as a soldier with, the Union. Aka *renegade* and *Tory*.

home guard: A local force organized for the protection of homes while the army was in a combat area.

homemade Yankee: Same as *homegrown Yankee* (q.v.).

homespun ball: In the South, an entertainment at which women wore dresses of coarse homespun.

Homestead Act: A United States congressional act of 1862, authorizing the distribution of free land to people who would live on the property for five years and cultivate it. Many soldiers protested that the best land would be gone before their enlistments ended.

hooker: A prostitute. Named after the Hook, a section of New York City known for its many brothels. The term was recorded by at least 1845.

Hooker's Division: In Washington, D.C., a prostitute district or the prostitutes in the district. So named because of General Joseph Hooker's reputation for frequenting brothels. By pure chance, the general's name coincided with the recently developed slang term *hooker* (q.v.).

hopper mine: A popular term for a rapid-fire gun with a hopperlike cartridge feeder.

hop, step, and jump: Any one of the early two-wheeled ambulances. So called because they bounced so wildly.

horizontal refreshment: Sexual intercourse.

horological torpedo: A *torpedo* (q.v.) set off through a timekeeping device, i.e., a time bomb. *Horological* means "pertaining to a timepiece." Besides using this formal term for the weapon, people also referred to it in simpler ways, such as "clock-work torpedo."

hors de combat: Disabled. French for "out of combat." Used in English since the mid-1700s.

horse collar: A blanket roll with the ends tied together. A soldier would sling it over one shoulder and rest it under the opposite arm.

hospital buzzard: A malingerer who extended his hospital stay far beyond a reasonable time. Aka *hospital rat*.

hospital rat: Same as *hospital buzzard* (q.v.).

hospital tent: Any tent used for hospital purposes, usually a *wall tent* (q.v.). The term had been used since at least the early 1800s.

hospital train: A train with specially fitted railway cars for transporting wounded soldiers.

housewife: A small sewing kit with needles, thread, and related items. A soldier had to repair his own uniform, so he commonly carried a sewing kit, which was unissued and had to be obtained privately. The term had been in civilian use since at least the mid-1700s.

how come you so: Liquor. This term had been used since the early 1800s as an adjective meaning intoxicated.

hunky: Fine, in good condition. This term became a popular slang expression just as the war was beginning. The word evolved from English dialectal *hunk* ("home base" in children's games), itself from Dutch *honk* ("home base"). Late in the war, or just after the war, the term expanded to *hunky-dory*.

I

IC: (1) An official marking by a Union government inspector, meaning that an item was "Inspected Condemned," i.e., unfit for service. Later the playful troops used the initials as a humorous byword. (2) An abbreviation for *Invalid Corps* (q.v.). Soldiers sometimes taunted a member of the Invalid Corps by calling him an IC with the obvious intention of meaning "Inspected Condemned."

I.F.W.: An abbreviation of *In For the War*.

impress into service, to: To steal. A humorous soldiers' application of the military-naval meaning (in use since the sixteenth century) to take by force for public service.

income tax: A tax on incomes. Before the Civil War, some states had an income tax. But it was the war that caused the United States Congress to establish the first Federal income tax in 1861. Later the Confederacy set up a similar tax.

in detail: By the engagement of small sections of a force one after another. Often in the phrase *to defeat in detail*, to defeat (a force) unit by unit, a process usually resulting from individual regiments or companies not being within supporting distance of each other. *Detail* had been recorded in variants of these expressions since at least the 1840s.

in echelon: See *echelon*.

infernal machine: Any kind of hidden explosive device. The term had been in use since at least the early 1800s.

In God We Trust: A motto on United States money. First authorized by Congress in 1864 for a two-cent bronze coin.

inspector general: An officer who investigated and reported on the army's organizational matters, such as morale, supplies, discipline, and finances. The title had been in use since at least the early 1700s.

intelligent contraband: Same as *contraband* (q.v.).

in the air: In the open country without protection (such as a river or a fortification) against a flank attack.

Invalid Corps: A Union corps of men who had been disabled by wounds or disease and were assigned to light duties as clerks, cooks, nurses, and so on. It was established in 1863. The following year it was renamed the *Veteran Reserve Corps*, largely because its initials, IC, provoked an unfortunate association with the government's "Inspected Condemned" stamp on worn-out equipment and animals. See also *IC* (1) and (2).

ironclad: (1) A naval vessel sheathed in iron armor. The term was used as an adjective, as in "ironclad ship," in the 1850s. When the Civil War prompted the building of many such vessels, the name was simplified to ironclad. (2) A humorous term for hardtack.

ironclad fever (iron fever): In the North, a period of intense belief in, and construction of, ironclads. Cf. *Monitor fever*.

ironclad life preserver: Same as *iron stove* (q.v.).

ironclad oath: The stringent oath of office that the United States Congress prescribed in 1862 for civilian and military officeholders. The oath aimed to exclude from office anyone who had participated in the rebellion. Its greatest impact came when it was applied during Reconstruction.

iron doughnut: Same as *Sherman's hairpin* (q.v.).

iron fever: Same as *ironclad fever* (q.v.).

iron foundry: An artillery missile.

iron stove: An iron vest, supposedly bulletproof, sold to recruits by private dealers early in the war. Soldiers commonly poked fun at someone wearing such a vest as being the *man in the iron stove*, a verbal play on the Man in the Iron Mask, the name of a mysterious person who spent forty years in French prisons and always wore a black velvet (not iron) mask when moving from prison to prison; the prisoner died in 1703, but he was still well known in the mid-1800s as a character in a novel by Alexandre Dumas. Aka *ironclad life preserver*.

irrepressible conflict: (1) The conflict between freedom and slavery. This sense of the expression was recorded before the war. (2) The Civil War.

itch: See *camp itch*.

jackass gun: A nickname for the Ellsworth gun because of its small size.

James projectile: An explosive artillery projectile invented by Senator Charles T. James of Rhode Island just before the war. It could be used in any cannon specially rifled for it. James also perfected a rifled cannon and a cylindrical bullet with a conical head.

James River fever: The fever contracted during the Peninsula campaign of 1862.

jayhawker: (1) A member of the antislavery bands in the irregular war fought in the 1850s to determine if Kansas would be a free or slave state. The origin of the term is uncertain. One theory is that the expression referred to a fictitious Kansas bird, the jayhawk, which combined the thieving qualities of the jay and the ferocious qualities of the hawk. However, the word seems to have originated in the Middle West or California as early as 1849, when it was reportedly used by a Galesburg, Illinois, party of goldseekers who went to the West Coast. (2) During the Civil War, a free-lance soldier or guerrilla in Kansas or elsewhere. (3) Any lawless marauder. (4) A Southern sympathizer in Kansas. This sense was a reversal of the original meaning of the word in that state.

Jeff Davis box (Jeff Davis' box): A creaking, ill-built military wagon in the Confederate army. Aka *musical box*.

Jeff Davis bread: Same as *ramrod bread* (q.v.).

Jeff Davis coffee: Wheat used as a coffee substitute by Southerners.

Jeff Davis hat: Same as *Hardee hat* (q.v.).

Jeff Davis money: Confederate money.

Jeff Davis necktie (Jeff Davis' necktie): Same as *Sherman's hairpin* (q.v.).

Jeffdom: The Confederate States of America. The term refers, of course, to President Jefferson Davis.

Jefferson boot: A boot or shoe that rose to about the ankle. The Jefferson boot was similar to the *ankle boot* (q.v.), but the Jefferson boot had a single thong, whereas the ankle boot had several eyelets for lacing.

Jeffite: A follower of Jefferson Davis. The word is usually seen as an attributive, as in "Jeffite traitors."

Jenifer saddle: A saddle with a flat, English-style seat, patented in 1860 by Walter H. Jenifer of Baltimore.

jigadier brindle: Same as *gigadier breneral* (q.v.).

Joe Brown's pets: The Georgia militia. So nicknamed because of Governor Joseph E. Brown's efforts to keep them from Confederate military service.

Joe Brown's pike: A weapon consisting of a blade atop a long staff. It was promoted by Governor Joseph E. Brown of Georgia, primarily for use by his state militia. Sometimes it was equipped with a curved hook called a *bridle cutter*, which was used to pull a man from his horse. The pike was never used in combat.

John Brown: An attributive meaning honoring, or in tribute to, the abolitionist John Brown, as in "a John Brown raid."

Johnny Reb (Johnny): A Confederate soldier. See also *Reb*.

Johns tent-knapsack: A knapsack that could hold a soldier's kit or open into a shelter tent. Patented in 1859 by William B. Johns of the United States Army.

Joint Committee on the Conduct of the War: See *Committee on the Conduct of the War*.

Jonah: Someone believed to bring bad luck. Many outfits seemed to have such a character. Based on the biblical Jonah, the term had long been used in the civilian world.

Josh: A Confederate soldier from Arkansas. Short for Joshua.

junk (salt junk): A sailors' term for salted meat. The word had been used with this meaning since at least the mid-1700s. It originated as a transferred sense of *junk* meaning old rope (which is what the salted meat must have tasted like).

K

katydid: A teenage soldier in the Southern army. Veteran Rebels applied the term in allusion to the insect's green color, *green* having a long history of meaning "immature" and "inexperienced." The word is best known for being applied to the Virginia Military Institute cadets who fought at the Battle of New Market, Virginia, in 1864.

Kearny Cross and Kearny Medal: Union army decorations named for Major General Philip Kearny, killed in 1862. The Medal, in 1862, was awarded to officers who had served under him. In 1863 the Cross was established for his enlisted men.

Kearny patch: A two-inch square patch of red flannel sewn onto the hat of each man under the command of the Union's Philip Kearny. The patches, which he had ordered so that he could distinguish his men in the field, soon led to the first official assignment of corps badges on a wide scale.

keg hat: A nickname for the regulation black felt full dress hat.

keg torpedo: See *torpedo*.

kepi: Any of various fatigue or forage caps with a visor and a round flat top, originally inspired by a French military cap known as a *képi*. An informal term that covered many specific kinds of headgear, such as the *McClellan cap* (q.v.).

Ketchum hand grenade: A hand grenade patented in 1861 by William F. Ketchum and issued to the Union army and navy.

Kilpatrick's monument: A blackened chimney standing alone in the rubble of a burned-down building. Named after Hugh Judson Kilpatrick, an aggressive Union officer under Sherman during the latter's march through the South in 1864-65. Cf. *Sherman's monument* and *Sherman's sentinel*.

K.G.C. Abbreviation for *Knights of the Golden Circle* (q.v.).

knapsack drill: (1) A soldiers' term for the preparations for, and holding of, an elaborate Sunday inspection of personnel, equipment, quarters, and so on. Soldiers even had to open their knapsacks so that officers could check the contents, hence the name. (2) A form of punishment in which a soldier had to march for a specified time or distance with his knapsack filled with heavy objects, such as bricks, rocks, or cannon balls.

Knights of the Golden Circle (Knights of the Circle, Golden Circle): A pro-Southern organization founded in the mid-1850s in Cincinnati to advocate the annexation of Mexico for the extension of slavery. During the Civil War, the founder of the society, George Bickley, lived in the South, but some pro-Southern Northerners adopted the name of his society and advocated the Southern cause. Similar or related societies included the *Order of American Knights* and the *Sons of Liberty*.

knock-'em-stiff (nockum stiff): Strong, especially home-made, liquor.

L

L: A quartermasters' symbol meaning "Lost in the service." Soldiers uttered the letter with an ironic wink, figuring that the symbol probably covered up a theft.

Ladies' Aid Society: A Northern women's organization that sent clothing, bandages, and other items to soldiers. See also *woman's aid society*.

ladies' gunboat: See *ladies' gunboat society*.

ladies' gunboat society: An organization of Southern women who raised funds to build ironclads. The first society was established in New Orleans in 1861, with others soon following elsewhere. Ladies' gunboat societies collected money by sponsoring many events, the best-known type being the *gunboat fair*, a fair whose proceeds went toward the ships. A *ladies' gunboat* was an ironclad built with funds from the societies.

Laird Rams: Two vessels with iron rammers extending seven feet beyond their prows. Contracted by the Confederates and built by John Laird and Son in England, the ships were seized by the British government for violating

Great Britain's neutrality laws and thus never saw action in the Civil War.

lame duck: An officeholder not reelected, especially a defeated member of the short session of Congress after a November election. Before the Civil War, the term had been used in other senses, such as a British stockbrocker who had lost his money.

lamppost: An artillery missile.

landlady: Same as *madam* (q.v.).

landsman: A naval recruit who had no previous experience on the sea. The term had long been so used.

lark: A foraging expedition. This was a wartime application of a word that had previously (since at least the early 1800s) designated any playful adventure.

Latin Farmer: Any one of many German immigrants who had fled the 1840s European revolutions and, though well educated in such topics as Latin and Greek, had become farmers in America through necessity. Several became Civil War generals, including the Union's Carl Schurz.

layout: A skulker, especially one who hid in the woods.

League: Short for *Union League* (q.v.).

League of Loyal Confederates: A civilian group set up in Mobile, Alabama, to promote support for Southern soldiers' morale late in the war.

leatherhead: One who was not a *copperhead* (q.v.).

Legal Tender Acts: A series of Union legislation authorizing paper currency, beginning in 1862. The resulting Treasury notes were popularly called greenbacks and were created to help finance the war.

liberty pin: An emblem worn by copperheads.

light draft: Same as *tinclad* (q.v.).

light twelve-pounder: Same as *Napoleon gun* (q.v.).

Lincoln coffee: A Southern term for Northern, or "real," coffee, as distinguished from the many substitutes (such as sweet potatoes) in the South, where coffee was scarce.

Lincolndom: A Southern nickname for the North. Cf. *Davisdom* Cf.

Lincoln flag: A Southern term for the Union flag.

Lincoln gimlet: Same as *Sherman's hairpin* (q.v.).

Lincoln government: A government in a state restored to the Union under President Lincoln's Reconstruction plans, which were more generous than those that would characterize Reconstruction after Lincoln's death. Lincoln restored Louisiana, for example.

Lincoln hireling: A Southern term for a Federal soldier.

Lincolnism: A Southern term for the political principles and policies of President Lincoln.

Lincolnite: (1) A supporter of the political principles and policies of President Lincoln. (2) A Union soldier or sympathizer. Both senses were used primarily in the South.

Lincoln navy: A Southern term for the Union navy.

Lincoln pie: A Union soldiers' term for a government-issued hardtack cracker.

Lincoln Plan: President Lincoln's Reconstruction plan as demonstrated in his restoration of Louisiana, Tennessee, and Arkansas. An essential feature was the requirement that one-tenth of the state's qualified voters of 1860 take an oath of loyalty to the Constitution. Aka *Louisiana Plan* and *One-tenth Plan*. See also *Lincoln government*.

Lincoln platform: Same as *Lincoln pie* (q.v.).

Lincoln pup: A Southern term for a Union soldier.

Lincoln rifle: Any of the thousands of shoulder arms provided to pro-Unionist home-guard units in Kentucky during the spring 1861 struggle to determine whether that state would secede from the United States.

Lincoln shingle: Same as *Lincoln pie* (q.v.).

Lincoln spy: A Union spy.

Lincoln troops: Union troops.

Lindsay rifle-musket: A muzzleloading weapon patented by John P. Lindsay in 1860. It fired two shots simultaneously, one loaded on top of the other. The Union used some Lindsays during the war.

line of battle: The position of ships or troops arranged for attack or defense. The expression had been used for ships since the 1600s and for ground forces since at least the early 1800s.

little coot: A Confederate name for a Yankee.

lobscouse (scouse): A stew consisting of meat, vegetables, and hardtack. Originally a sailor's dish (going back to at least the early 1700s), but adopted by soldiers as well. The origin of the term is obscure.

Loggerhead: A Union soldier from Pennsylvania.

long taw: Long range, said of artillery fire. The term was borrowed from the civilian expression *at long taw*, meaning at a distance, which in turn came from the game of marbles, a taw being a shooter or the line from which shots were made.

Long Tom: A nickname for any of various guns of large size and long range. The term had been in use since at least the 1830s.

loose bowels: A doctor. Soldiers' slang.

Lost Order: A copy of General Lee's field order detailing his plans for capturing Harper's Ferry, Virginia (later in West Virginia), dated September 9, 1862, lost by a Southern courier or officer, and found by a Union soldier. However, the North, under General McClellan, gained little profit from the document.

Louisiana firewater: Whiskey issued to Northern troops in Louisiana.

Louisiana Plan: Same as *Lincoln Plan* (q.v.).

loyal: Faithful to the Union.

loyalist: A Union sympathizer, North or South. The term had been used during the American Revolution to signify one who favored the British.

loyal league: A type of Northern organization formed to stimulate loyalty to the Union. Loyal leagues, known generically as the *Union League of America*, were set up throughout the North. Late in the war, and just after the war, some leagues went South and underground to organize freedmen politically.

loyal leaguer: A member of a *loyal league* (q.v.).

M

McClellan: Short for *McClellan cap* (q.v.), *McClellan saddle* (q.v.), and *McClellan tree* (q.v.).

McClellan cap: A forage cap modeled after the true French képi and differing from the regulation cap by having a lower crown, among other features. The cap was a rage in 1862, but the color tended to fade, so it lost its appeal among the men. It was, however, favored by McClellan (hence the name) and some other officers.

McClellan pie: A Union soldiers' term for an army-issued hardtack cracker.

McClellan saddle: A saddle modeled on a Hungarian style and designed by George B. McClellan in the 1850s. Rugged, it was the best of several used in the Civil War.

McClellan tree: Same as *McClellan saddle* (q.v.).

madam (madame): A female owner or manager of a brothel. This term had been in use since the late 1600s, but it was the Civil War, which took thousands of farm boys into the big cities, that made the word familiar to the American masses. Aka *landlady*.

mail boy: A man who collected and distributed mail. Though the term had been used since at least the early 1840s, it was the Civil War that put the expression on everyone's lips. In the Union army, the mail boy was an officer who delivered mail to the soldiers.

make a cathole, to: To shoot someone.

man in the iron stove: See *iron stove*.

March to the Sea: The Union army's drive from Atlanta to Savannah, during November and December 1864, led by William Tecumseh Sherman, who split the South and largely destroyed its resources.

marine, to play (someone) for a: To fool (someone). This expression was based on the long-held belief that a marine would believe anything. In the early 1800s, an ignorant seaman was called a *marine*, and by 1806 people were saying *tell that to the marines* (i.e., the marines will believe a tall tale, but not the sailors).

Medal of Honor: The highest decoration for valor in the United States Army and Navy. Congress authorized the award for naval enlisted men in December 1861, army enlisted personnel in July 1862, and army officers in March 1863 (naval officers had to wait till the twentieth century). Later usually called the *Congressional Medal of Honor*.

military governor: A military officer who administered the civil or executive affairs of a state or region occupied by military forces.

Military Telegraph (United States Military Telegraph): The Federal communications system set up, at the government's request, by American Telegraph Company and Western Union Telegraph Company in 1862.

militia: A military force liable to call only in an emergency. The term had been used with various meanings since the sixteenth century.

millish: Short for *militia* (q.v.).

Minié ball (Minié bullet, minnie, etc.): (1) Though usually referred to as a "ball" during the Civil War, actually an elongated rifle-musket projectile with a hollow base that, on firing, expanded into the grooves of the barrel and spun from the muzzle, giving the bullet greater force and accuracy than was possible with traditional musket balls. It was developed in the 1840s by the French army officers Henri-Gustave Delvigne and Claude-Etienne Minié. Soldiers' mispronunciation of *Minié* accounted for the spelling *minnie*. (2) Hence, in soldiers' lingo, any projectile fired from a rifled musket.

Minié rifle (Minié, etc.): A rifled shoulder arm capable of firing the *Minié ball* (q.v.).

Minié rifle whiskey (Minié rifle, minnie rifle, etc.): A cheap, strong whiskey. The term was recorded by at least 1858, but it was most widely used during the Civil War.

minuteman: A member of any of various Southern groups ready to resist enemy forces at a minute's notice. The term, widely used in the days just before the outbreak of hostilities, was adopted from its similar use during the American Revolution.

miscegenation: The mixture of races by intermarriage or cohabitation, especially between a white person and a black. Apparently the word was coined by David Goodman Croly, of New York City, in a pamphlet entitled *Miscegenation: The Theory of the Blending of the Races, Applied to the American White Man and Negro* (copyrighted 1863, published anonymously 1864). *Miscegenation* is based on a combination of Latin *miscere* ("to mix") and genus ("race"). Related words quickly evolved, such as *miscegenist, to miscegenate*, and *miscegenated*. Cf. *subgenation*.

Mississippi butternut: A Confederate soldier from Mississippi.

monitor: Any Union ironclad modeled after the U.S.S. *Monitor*, i.e., a heavily armored warship having a low freeboard and one or more revolving turrets with guns.

monitor fever: (1) The enthusiasm that swept the North after the U.S.S. *Monitor* proved equal to the challenge of the C.S.S. *Virginia* (formerly the Northern frigate *Merrimack*) when the ironclads battled off Hampton Roads, Virginia, in March 1862. Specifically, the rush to build more ironclads during that period of enthusiasm. Cf. *ironclad fever*. (2) A kind of ship's fever said to be prevalent among sailors under the strain of blockade duty on *monitor* (q.v.) warships.

mortar boat: A gunboat with mounted mortars. Related terms popularized during the Civil War include *mortar fleet*, *mortar raft*, *mortar schooner*, and *mortar vessel*.

Mosbyite: A guerrilla fighter under Confederate Colonel John S. Mosby.

mossyback (mossback): Someone who hid from the war, presumably in a remote forest, where moss would grow on his back. The term was most common in the South, often in the expression *mossybacked ranger*. Sometimes seen in print as *mossybank*, probably because of an early typographical error that had been perpetuated.

Mr. Lincoln's gun: A nickname for the Spencer carbine/rifle. President Lincoln took a personal interest in making the weapon available to the Union army.

mud lark: A farmer's pig clandestinely killed and eaten by troops. This meaning was a new twist on *mud lark*, which since the early 1800s in America had designated any hog. The term originated as British slang c. 1780. Aka *possum*, *slow bear*, and *slow deer*.

Mud March: The attempt of the Union's Army of the Potomac, led by Ambrose E. Burnside, to move across the Rappahannock River and seize Confederate positions in January 1863, doomed to failure by a heavy rain that made roads impassable. Coupled with Burnside's defeat at Fredericksburg the previous December, the embarrassment of the Mud March (so termed even in official reports) resulted in his being relieved of command.

mudscow: A soldiers' humorous term for a broad army shoe. The word had previously designated a large flat-bottomed barge.

mudsill: A derisive Southern term for a Northerner. In 1858 the term had been coined by Senator J.H. Hammond of South Carolina to designate a member of the laboring classes. Also in 1858 the term was applied to any Democrat who espoused popular sovereignty.

mule: (1) A heavy, clumsy European musket purchased early in the war. The weapon had a kick like a mule. Aka *pumpkin slinger* (q.v.). (2) Bad meat or salt beef.

mule cavalry: A humorous name for mounted infantry.

mule litter: An American term for the French cacolet, a device for transporting wounded from the field by mule or horse.

multiform: A ragged uniform. A sarcastic term used by tattered Confederate soldiers.

musical box: Same as Jeff Davis box (q.v.).

musket: A heavy smoothbore shoulder firearm. The term originated in the sixteenth century.

musket shell: A bullet that could explode after entering the body. Aka explosive bullet.

mustered out, to be: Figuratively, to be killed in action.

muster in, to: (1) To assemble (a watch) when going on duty. (2) (muster into, to) To enroll (a recruit) into the military service.

muster out, to: To discharge (someone) from the service.

N

Napoleon gun (Napoleon): A smoothbore field artillery piece. Named for Napoleon III, a patron of its development in France in the mid-1850s. Little used in America till the Civil War, when it became a basic weapon on both sides. Aka gun howitzer and light twelve-pounder.

National: (1) (noun) A Union soldier. (2) (adjective) Belonging to the Union, as in "National troops."

national bank: Any one of the many Union commercial banks chartered under the banking acts of 1863-64 to issue currency notes and provide other services.

National Banking Law: An 1863 law enacted by the United States Congress establishing the national banking system.

national banking system: The framework of national banks formed under the National Banking Law of 1863.

National Covenant: A society organized by Northern women who pledged that, during the war, they would not purchase any foreign article when an American one could be substituted.

National Flag, Confederate: The flag adopted in 1863 to replace the *Stars and Bars* (q.v.). In the upper left corner was a small version of the *Battle Flag* (q.v.); the rest of the flag was white. In early 1865 the National Flag was revised to include a vertical red bar on the right edge. Aka *Stainless Banner*.

National Union party: Same as *Union party* (q.v.).

Naval Jack: A Confederate navy flag authorized by Stephen R. Mallory, secretary of the navy, in 1863. It was a modified form of the *Battle Flag* (q.v.).

Negro brogan: A term often used in Federal contracts with shoe manufacturers, possibly for a type of army shoe resembling that worn by blacks on plantations.

Negro bureau (nigger bureau): A familiar name for the *Freedman's Bureau* (q.v.).

Negro cloth: Same as *nigger cloth* (q.v.).

Negrohead: Same as *niggerhead* (q.v).

Negro Soldier Law: A law, signed by President Jefferson Davis in 1865, that authorized the formation of companies of black soldiers for the Confederacy. However, the war ended before the black troops could participate.

New Ensign: A Confederate navy flag authorized by Secretary of the Navy Mallory in 1863. It was a reduced version of the first *National Flag* (q.v.).

new regular: A man who enlisted in the Union's regular army after the war began. Cf. *old regular.*

news walkers: Soldiers who, on their own initiative, carried news from campfire to campfire.

New York Stock Exchange: The new name for the New York Stock and Exchange Board when it moved to its present location at Broad and Wall streets during the financial boom of the Civil War.

nigger baby: Any of the large projectiles fired into Charleston, South Carolina, by the Union's Quincy A. Gillmore during his siege of that city in 1863. The term was coined by P.G.T. Beauregard, the Confederate commander in charge of defending Charleston. See also *Swamp Angel.*

nigger bureau: Same as *Negro bureau* (q.v.).

nigger cloth (Negro cloth): Another name for *butternut cloth* (q.v.). The term, in use since at least the 1730s, referred to the fact that slaves often wore the cloth.

niggerhead (Negrohead): A copperhead term for Union men advocating violent measures to resolve the slavery issue. Hence *niggerheadism,* the belief in such measures. Aka *nigger worshiper* (2). Cf. *nigger worshiper* (1).

nigger war: A term for the Civil War widely used among Union soldiers after the *Emancipation Proclamation* (q.v.).

nigger worshiper: (1) One who favored abolition or showed an interest in the welfare of blacks. The term originated just before the war and was widely used during the conflict. (2) Same as *niggerhead* (q.v.).

night blindness: A defect of vision characterized by little or no ability to see at night, though daytime sight may be normal. Many Confederate soldiers complained of this malady, which may have been brought about by a combination of excessive exposure to sunlight, dietary deficiencies, and exhaustion. The term had been used since at least the mid-1700s. Aka *gravel* (q.v.).

ninety-day gunboat: Any of the heavily armed gunboats quickly built by the Union early in the war.

nockum stiff: Same as *knock-'em-stiff* (q.v.).

North: The states, and/or the population of the states, remaining in the United States after the secession of the states forming the Southern Confederacy. Before the Civil War, the word had a geographical denotation, referring to the land or the people of the northern part of the United States. With the war came the political sense of the term.

Northern Republic: The Northern states in the Civil War.

Northwest Conspiracy: A plan that Northern officials claimed was formulated by Confederate agents in Canada and was aimed at using members of the *Sons of Liberty* (q.v.) to create a *Northwestern Confederacy* (q.v.).

Northwestern Confederacy: A supposedly planned, but never formed, government unifying the northwestern part of the United States (including Illinois), to be initiated by a revolution incited by Southern sympathizers. See also *Northwest Conspiracy*.

not on your tintype: See *tintype*.

noxious effluvia: A medical term for camp odors that doctors believed could make soldiers ill.

O

o-be-joyful (O-be-joyful, Oh, Be Joyful, etc.): Hard liquor. The expression was borrowed from England in the early 1800s.

oblique order: An order to attack *in echelon* (see *echelon*).

oil of gladness: Hard liquor.

old bull: Another name for tough *salt horse* (q.v.).

old gridiron: The Union flag. A contemptuous name applied by Southern women.

old horse: Corned beef.

old man: A playful name adopted by one or the other of the two soldiers in a dog tent. Cf. *old woman*.

old quinine: Same as *quinine* (q.v.).

old red-eye: Same as *red-eye* (q.v.).

old regular: A man who enlisted in the Union's Regular Army before the war. Cf. *new regular*.

old soldier: An experienced soldier, especially one who knew how to avoid special duty. Before the war, the same term was used in its literal meaning as well as a wide variety of extended senses.

old woman: A playful name adopted by one or the other of the two soldiers in a dog tent. There were no sexual implications in this designation. Cf. *old man*.

old wristbreaker: Same as *wristbreaker* (q.v.).

onion day: In the North, a school day for collecting produce for the army. Cf. *potato day*.

One-tenth Plan: Same as *Lincoln Plan* (q.v.).

On to Richmond/Washington!: Same as *Forward to Richmond/Washington!* (q.v.).

open the ball, to: To start a battle.

opium pills: A soldiers' derogatory name for a surgeon.

Order of American Knights: See *Knights of the Golden Circle*.

Order of the Heroes of America: See *Heroes of America, Order of the*.

ordinance of secession: An enactment passed by a representative body of a state to express that state's intention to withdraw from the Union. Aka *secession ordinance*.

ordnance gun: A rifled *Rodman gun* (q.v.) developed by the Union's ordnance department in 1863.

owls: A facetious term for imaginary creatures who "captured" soldiers at night. A fanciful way of accounting for desertion. When a man slipped away under cover of darkness, it was said that "the owls got him."

P

Pacific Confederacy: A projected confederacy on the Pacific Coast. Cf. *Pacific Republic*.

Pacific Railway Act (Railroad Act): An act authorizing America's first transcontinental railroad, passed by Congress and signed by President Lincoln in 1862.

Pacific Republic: A proposed new country to be formed in the region west of the Rockies, supported by Southern sympathizers, especially in California. The name and idea had been around since the 1840s. Cf. *Pacific Confederacy*.

paleface: A new recruit.

panada: A hot gruel, usually consisting of cornmeal, mashed hardtack, wine, and ginger boiled in water. Created by Eliza Harris of the Sanitary Commission and used in Union army hospitals. The word *panada* (borrowed from Spanish and based on a root meaning "bread") had, since the sixteenth century, designated a dish of boiled bread flavored to taste. The Civil War panada aka *bully soup* (q.v.) and *ginger panada*.

paper blockade: A blockade proclaimed but not backed up by force. Early in the Civil War, the Northern blockade of Southern ports was called a paper blockade because the Union navy was too small to be effective. The term had been in use since at least the early 1800s.

parlor house: An expensive brothel with a parlor.

parole: A pledge by a prisoner of war that, if released, he would not take up arms against his captors till he was formally exchanged for a prisoner from the other side. The term, from the French *parole d'honneur* ("parole of honor"), had been in use since the seventeenth century.

parole camp: A camp for holding parolees till they were regularly exchanged.

Parrott gun: A rifled, muzzleloading, cast-iron cannon of varying caliber, characterized by a breech reinforced with a band of wrought iron. Robert Parker Parrott patented the design in October 1861. The *Parrott gun* and the *Parrott projectile* (q.v.) greatly helped the Union side in the war.

Parrott projectile: An improved expanding projectile, ranging from ten to 300 pounds, for rifled ordnance. Robert Parker Parrott patented the design in August 1861.

partisan ranger: A member of a Southern band of irregulars engaged in guerrilla warfare to harass the enemy and to capture goods for which they would be paid by the Confederate government. The Confederacy authorized such bands in 1862. The most famous partisan ranger was

John Singleton Mosby. Since the 1600s, the word partisan had designated a similar kind of soldier.

patent bureau (bureau): A soldiers' slang term for a knapsack, which often held all sorts of miscellaneous items.

Peace and Constitutional Society (Peace and Constitutional Union Society): One of three principal Southern groups opposed to secession. See also *Heroes of America, Order of the* and *Peace Society*.

Peace Conference/Convention: Same as *Border Slave State Convention* (q.v.).

Peace Democrat: In the North, a Democratic party member who opposed the Civil War and urged peaceful measures. Opponents called such a person a *copperhead* (q.v.).

Peace Society: One of three principal Southern groups opposed to secession. See also *Heroes of America, Order of the* and *Peace and Constitutional Society*.

peas on a trencher: A soldiers' nickname for breakfast call. A trencher was a platter for serving food.

peddle lead, to: To shoot repeatedly and quickly.

penitentiary uniform: A derogatory term for some early Northern uniforms made of shoddy material.

Pennant: A Confederate navy flag authorized by Secretary of the Navy Mallory in 1863. It was a banner one foot wide at the head, tapering seventy-two feet to a point.

People's Union ticket: At the beginning of the war, a list of candidates who supported the United States government despite political differences, as distinguished from candidates who supported it as adherents.

Petersburg Express: Same as *Dictator* (q.v.).

picket: A single soldier or a small detachment of troops guarding an army from a surprise attack. The term had been in use since at least the mid-1700s.

pickled mule: Salted meat.

pie eater: A man with a rural background. A term current among some Union soldiers.

pigeon shot: A Confederate term for a smoothbore projectile in which, after it cleared the muzzle, springs popped out a pair of triangular wings to stabilize the flight. The expression *pigeon shot* had previously designated small-sized bird shot.

pilot bread (pilot biscuit): Hardtack used aboard ship. The term *pilot bread* had been in use since at least the 1780s, *pilot biscuit* since the early 1800s.

pine top: Cheap whiskey, allegedly made from pine needles. A Southern expression first recorded just before the war.

play (someone) for a marine, to: See *marine, to play (someone) for a.*

play the white man, to: To be arrogant. The phrase was used by black troops to describe the attitude of some of their black noncommissioned officers.

Plymouth pilgrim: A derisive name in the South for a Northern soldier.

Pomeroy Circular: An anti-Lincoln letter circulated by Senator Samuel C. Pomeroy in early 1864. It touted Salmon P. Chase, secretary of the treasury, for the presidency.

poncho tent: A set of three rubberized ponchos convertible into a tent that would sleep three men.

pontoon: (1) A flat-bottomed boat or portable float used in large numbers to support a floating temporary bridge. The word, borrowed from French *ponton* ("floating bridge"), had been in use since the 1600s but did not become commonplace in America till the Civil War brought about the need for many pontoon bridges. (2) A Yankee name for a broad army shoe.

pony: A boy soldier. The word *pony* had designated a small horse since the seventeenth century.

Pook turtles: Seven Federal ironclad gunboats designed by Samuel M. Pook. Because they were named after river ports (such as Cincinnati and Louisville), the ships were also referred to as *city class*. Aka *Eads ironclads* because they were built by James Eads.

popskull: Inferior, especially homemade, liquor. Cf. *busthead*.

possum: Same as *mud lark* (q.v.).

postage currency (postage-stamp currency): The official name of the August 1862 issue of *fractional currency* (q.v.), consisting of facsimiles of current postage stamps. This currency was a short-lived stopgap between *stamp money* (q.v.) and true fractional bills.

postage stamp: During the Civil War, a term that often designated a gummed or ungummed stamp used as *stamp money* (q.v.), or a piece of *postage currency* (q.v.), in addition to its primary meaning (since the 1840s) as an indicator of prepayment of a mailing fee.

postal currency: Same as *postage currency* (q.v.).

potato day: In the North, a school day for collecting produce for the army. Cf. *onion day*.

Potomac chowder: A dish made by burning hardtack, boiling it in water.

powder boat: A vessel that, in December 1864, Union forces loaded with gunpowder and detonated (by time fuses) offshore near Fort Fisher in North Carolina. The purpose was to damage the fort, but the project failed completely.

"Prayer of Twenty Millions, The": A public letter to President Lincoln, written by Horace Greeley and published in his *New York Tribune* in August 1862, in which Greeley, in the name of twenty million Northerners, argued that Lincoln should end slavery.

preliminary Emancipation Proclamation: President Lincoln's September 1862 announcement that the final *Emancipation Proclamation* (q.v.) would take effect on January 1, 1863. Lincoln himself used the words *preliminary* and *final* to describe the two documents.

presidential governor: A governor appointed by President Lincoln (or, later, by President Johnson) for a Southern state.

pretty rapid little case: A loose woman. Cf. *fast trick.*

prison pen: A penlike prison. A Civil War term to describe prisoner-of-war camps.

prize: A ship or other property captured at sea in war. The term had been so used since at least the early 1500s.

Prize Cases: United States Supreme Court cases, adjudicated in 1863, that upheld President Lincoln's seizure of certain ships for violating the Northern blockade in the early months of the war.

Proclamation of Amnesty and Reconstruction: President Lincoln's proclamation asserting his conditions for restoring Southern citizens and states to the Union. The proclamation was actually two separate documents, both issued on December 8, 1863. The Proclamation of Amnesty offered conditional pardons to most Southern citizens (exceptions included civil officials and high-ranking military officers). Lincoln's political Reconstruction plans were embedded in his Annual Message to Congress.

Proclamation of Emancipation: A term for the Emancipation Proclamation before it was issued.

Proclamation of Thanksgiving: The name for each of several public announcements by President Lincoln. Some designated specific days for giving praise and prayers to God in thanks for military victories, such as one issued on July 15, 1863, setting aside August 6. However, the two of most lasting significance were issued in October 1863 and October 1864, each designating the last Thursday in November as a day of thanks for divine goodness, with minimal reference to military affairs. These became the first two of the annual presidential proclamations setting aside Thanksgiving Day as a national holiday. Before Lincoln, the holiday, since it started in Plymouth, Massachusetts, in 1621, had been celebrated sporadically and mostly regionally.

Produce Loan Act: An 1862 Confederate Congress statute that permitted planters to pay for government bonds with agricultural produce.

Provisional Army of the Confederate States: The Southern volunteer forces during the Civil War. Aka (informally) *Confederate army* (q.v.). Cf. *Army of the Confederate States of America*.

pulverized potatoes: Same as *desiccated potatoes* (q.v.).

pumpkin rinds: A Union soldiers' term for lieutenants or lieutenancies. So called because of the shape of the shoulder straps for that rank.

pumpkin slinger: An outmoded European musket purchased early in the war. The weapon was usually bulky enough to hurl a pumpkin. Aka *mule* (q.v.).

puny list: A Southern soldiers' mocking term for those on sick call.

pup tent: Another name for the *dog tent* (q.v.). Aka *doghouse, shelter tent,* and *tente d'abri* (q.v. all).

put on the roots, to be: To be assigned extra tours of guard duty as punishment. A Confederate soldiers' expression.

Q

Quaker gun (quaker): A dummy piece of artillery, usually a log painted black. So called because of the Quaker opposition to war. The term was recorded as early as 1809, but it first attained widespread familiarity when the South, because of its shortages during the Civil War, often had to resort to such "weapons."

Quaker gunboat: A sham gunboat, with logs made to look like guns. See also *Quaker gun.*

quarantined in camp: Restricted to camp for disciplinary reasons.

quartermaster hunting: The condition in which artillery fire passed over the battle line and landed so far behind it that the only people likely to be hit were quartermaster personnel.

quickstep: A Union soldiers' term for diarrhea or dysentery. The word was usually preceded by a qualifier naming the location where the soldiers were encamped when the affliction struck, e.g., *Tennessee quickstep* and *Virginia quickstep.*

quinine (old quinine): A soldiers' derogatory name for a doctor.

quinine and whiskey: A drink used as a tonic. Hospitalized soldiers became very familiar with it.

R

radical: A Northerner who favored extreme measures against the South, such as abolishing slavery and confiscating property. Hence *radicalism*, the political principles of the radicals.

Radical party: A name sometimes applied to the Republican party, especially its extremist element.

Radical Republican: A member of a Republican-party faction that rose to prominence during the Civil War by advocating an immediate emancipation of slaves and a punitive policy toward the South after the war.

rag out, to: To dress up.

raider: Among Union prisoners at the Andersonville, Georgia, prison, one of the thieves who terrorized fellow prisoners. Cf. *regulator*.

Railroad Act: See *Pacific Railway Act*.

railroad monitor: A large rifled gun mounted on an armored railroad car. Confederate usage made the weapon famous.

rail-splitter: A Lincoln supporter, especially in the 1860 campaign.

ram: A warship having a prow fitted with a heavy beak for piercing an enemy ship. It was the Civil War that popularized this kind of vessel.

ram fever: An exaggerated fear among Northerners that Southern ironclads would break through blockades and attack Northern coastal cities.

ramrod bread: Cornmeal plastered onto a rifle ramrod and cooked over a campfire. A Southern dish. Aka *Jeff Davis bread*. See also *cush*.

Rat Hell: At Libby Prison in Richmond, Virginia, a vermin-infested section of the cellar. So named by Northern prisoners as they used it as a base while they were tunneling out.

readmission: The restoration of any of the seceding Southern states to the Union. The term was recorded in this specific sense by at least 1864.

ready finder: A civilian who followed Union troops and picked up discarded items.

rear admiral: See *admiral*.

Reb: Short for *Rebel* (q.v.). See also *Johnny Reb*.

Rebel: (1) (noun) A Confederate civilian or soldier. In plural, the Confederacy or its military forces. (2) (adjective) Pertaining to the Southern Confederacy. The word appeared in many combinations, such as *Rebel band, Rebel regiment, Rebel camp,* and *Rebel steamer.* Distinctive examples follow.

Rebel army: The Confederate army.

Rebel conch: A usually derogatory term for a Southern white, especially one from the Florida keys.

Rebel Confederacy: The Southern Confederacy.

Rebeldom: The Confederate States of America.

Rebeless: A female rebel.

Rebel gray: The gray cloth used for Confederate soldiers' uniforms.

Rebelism: The feelings, beliefs, or actions of Confederates during the Civil War.

rebellionist: An advocate of the Southern cause.

Rebel prisoner: See *galvanized.*

Rebel rag: A Northern term for a Confederate flag.

Rebel state: One of the Confederate States of America.

Rebel yell: A characteristic yell given by Confederate soldiers as they were going into battle. Said to have been a prolonged, high-pitched sound, possibly based on Southern fox-hunting cries.

reconstruction: (1) The reorganization of the United States with the North subjugated to the South through the latter's revolutionary tactics. This sense of the term was used in 1861. (2) The reorganization and reestablishment of the seceded states in the Union. This meaning of the word was beginning to be widely used in 1863.

reconstructionist: A Southerner who advocated reorganizing the Southern social system so as to avoid civil strife. This sense of the term was used in 1861. (After the war, a Reconstructionist was an advocate of the Reconstruction policies of the United States Congress).

red-eye (old red-eye): Inferior whiskey. The term had been in use since at least the early 1800s.

redleg (red-legged scout): A member of a band of free-state guerrillas in Kansas. So called because they wore red leggings. In border conflicts, they served as Federal scouts.

red-legged infantry: A name sometimes given to *Zouave* (q.v.) and other regiments that wore fancy red trousers.

Red-String Band (Red Strings): Same as *Heroes of America, Order of the* (q.v.).

Reed projectile: An artillery projectile with a soft, hollow, cupped base that expanded on firing to fit the rifling of the weapon. Developed in the 1850s by a Dr. Reed of Alabama, the projectile was used mostly by the South.

refugee: During the Civil War, a person who left his or her home area to seek refuge in, or to aid the cause of, the other side. Since the seventeenth century, the term had designated one who, because of religious or political persecution at home, sought refuge in a foreign country.

refuse a flank, to: To hold back a flank of one's own force while the rest of the line makes contact with the enemy. The purpose was to freeze in place a number of the enemy's troops while a decisive attack was being launched against them from another side. The expression went back to at least the late 1700s.

Regular Army, Confederate States: Same as *Army of the Confederate States of America* (q.v.).

Regular Army, United States: The permanently organized standing army of the United States. Throughout the Civil War, this small force was kept as a separate service from the various volunteer armies, but individual Regulars were parceled out here and there to volunteer units.

regulator: Among Union prisoners at the Andersonville, Georgia, prison, one of the vigilantes who fought against criminals who victimized fellow inmates. Cf. *raider*.

Remington: The name of several types of small arms manufactured by the Remington Arms Company. The most important during the Civil War was a single-shot carbine patented in December 1863 and used by the Union. Remington revolvers, 1861 and 1863 models, also saw service during the war.

renegade: Same as *homegrown Yankee* (q.v.).

repentant Rebel: See *galvanized*.

Repertorial Corps: A name sometimes given to war correspondents when they repeated themselves too much. The term was based on a pun between *reportorial* (of a reporter) and *repertorial* (of a repertory company, one that regularly repeated a limited number of plays).

Requa battery (Requa rifle battery): A weapon with 25 barrels arranged horizontally and designed to fire 7 volleys (i.e., 175 shots) per minute. It was developed by the Billinghurst Company of Rochester, New York, in 1861. Aka *covered-bridge gun* because its multiple shots could stop an enemy charge across a bridge (many bridges at that time were "covered" with wooden roofs and sidewalls).

retrograde movement: Any movement of a command to the rear or away from the enemy. Not synonymous with retreat. The term had been used since at least the early 1800s.

re-union: The restoration of the South to the Union. The word was being so used by 1863.

revenue agent: A Federal official who aided in the prevention, detection, and punishment of frauds on the nation's internal revenue. The position was authorized by statutes created during the war.

revenue stamp: A government stamp affixed to a product to prove that a tax had been paid. See also *stamp money* and *stamped notes*.

revetment: A support or reinforcing wall. Sandbags, for example, could be used as revetments for fieldworks. Masonry revetments supported brick fortifications. The word, in use since at least the 1770s, was borrowed from French and is based on a root meaning "to clothe again."

revolutionist: One sympathetic to the Southern Confederacy.

rich man's war, poor man's fight: A common saying among soldiers. Both sides allowed wealthy draftees to hire substitutes. And Southern troops were particularly upset at the exemption of men who owned twenty (later fifteen) or more slaves.

rifle knock-knee: Hard liquor. A Southern term. Cf. *rifle whiskey*.

rifle-musket (rifled musket): A muzzleloading shoulder arm that had a rifled (spiral-grooved) barrel interior, but exterior dimensions and details characteristic of the old musket. The term was in use by at least the early 1840s.

rifle pit: A short, shallow trench facing the enemy, with the earth mound in front as a protection for the soldier, who lay in a prone firing position. The term appeared in print by at least the mid-1850s.

rifle whiskey: Cheap, inferior whiskey. A Southern term that was recorded by at least the mid-1850s. Cf. *rifle knock-knee*.

right on the goose, to be: See *goose question*.

roast beef: Lunch call.

Robbers Row: A soldiers' term for the sutler tents in a camp. Sutlers were notorious for skinning the troops.

rock me to sleep, mother: Whiskey.

Rodman gun: A gun cast with a hollow core and cooled from the inside. The process, which greatly strengthened many large guns used by the Union in the Civil War, was devised by Thomas J. Rodman, an officer in the United States Army in the 1840s, but was not officially adopted till 1859. The process was used on both smoothbores and rifled guns. See also *ordnance gun*.

Roll of Honor: A list of Confederate officers and soldiers who displayed courage during action in the Civil War. The South lacked the resources to give medals, so in October 1862 the Confederate Congress authorized, as a substitute, the Roll of Honor, published in Southern newspapers after each battle.

rotgut (rot, rotgut whiskey): Cheap, inferior whiskey. The term had been used in England since the late sixteenth century, usually referring to a kind of beer. In early nineteenth century America, the word became familiar as a designation for strong, stomach-burning whiskey.

rot of popskull: Inferior whiskey.

route step (route march): A manner of marching in which troops maintained prescribed formations and intervals but were not required to keep step or observe silence.

Roys and Lilliendahl rocket: A war rocket, probably the best of its time, patented in 1862 by the North's Thomas W. Roys and Gustavus A. Lilliendahl.

Rucker ambulance: The most dependable Union ambulance, a four-wheeler adopted near the end of the war.

rump congress: The United States Congress during the Civil War, in which there were no representatives from the Southern states. In England the word *rump* had designated the remnant of a political body since the mid-1600s. Aka *rump government*.

rump government: Same as *rump congress* (q.v.).

run a Mick (shove a Mick), to: Among soldiers in the Confederate army, to get an Irishman drunk, induce him to enlist, procure a huge fee from a wealthy draftee using the Irishman as a substitute, and then get the poor soul drunk again for the same trick with another client.

runner: (1) Same as crimp (q.v.). Before the war, *runner* had designated a solicitor or a bill collector. (2) A *blockade-runner* (q.v.).

run the blockade, to: To enter or leave a blockaded port by eluding the blockading force.

run the guard, to: To elude the guard, go AWOL. The expression had been used since at least the 1840s.

S

sack coat: A loose-fitting, four-button fatigue coat. The term had been used since at least the 1840s.

Salem cloth: Cloth made in Salem, Oregon, often used for military uniforms.

salt horse: Salted or pickled beef. Originally sailors' slang, the term had been recorded since at least the 1830s. Aka *old bull*.

salt junk: Same as *junk* (q.v.).

Sanitary Commission (United States Sanitary Commission): A civilian organization that helped the Union army care for sick and wounded soldiers and their families. Established in 1861, it was originally called the Commission of Inquiry and Advice in Respect of the Sanitary Interests of the United States Forces.

Sanitary fair: Any of various events to raise funds for the *Sanitary Commission* (q.v.). Among the activities were teas, parades, art shows, auctions, and old-fashioned sales of homemade pies, jellies, quilts, raffle chances, and so on. One special item sold at a Sanitary fair was President Lincoln's original copy of the Emancipation Proclamation.

sanitary fodder: A Union soldiers' term for *desiccated vegetables* (q.v.). The vegetables ("fodder") were issued to help prevent scurvy.

Sanitary potato patch: A garden raised by a farmer for the *Sanitary Commission*.

sap-roller: A large cylindrical basketwork rolled, as a protection against enemy fire, ahead of men digging a sap (trench). The term had been used since at least the 1830s.

sardine box: A shoulder strap.

satellite cruiser: A captured ship used by the Confederates for military operations against the Union.

sauerkraut (sour crout, sour kraut, etc.): A German-American soldier during the Civil War. Named, of course, after the German fermented cabbage called sauerkraut. A German had been so called in the United States since at least the early 1840s.

Savage revolver: A revolver with two triggers, patented in 1860 by Edward Savage. The Union army used it on a limited basis.

sawbones: Slang term for a surgeon. The expression had been recorded since at least the 1830s.

scalawag: A white Republican in the South. Before the war, the term had meant a scamp.

scorpion bile: Inferior whiskey.

scouse: A shortened form of *lobscouse* (q.v.).

scout: (1) A Confederate spy wearing his own army's uniform. (2) In either army, one who went out ahead of the main force to observe enemy positions and movements. This sense of the term went back to the sixteenth century.

screen: Anything that shielded or protected a force from the enemy, such as a parapet of earth or a small unit of troops detached to cover a larger body.

scyugle, to: See *skiugle, to*.

sea pie: A usually multilayered dish of meat and crust. Familiar since at least the mid-1700s.

seceded state: One of the Southern states that seceded from the Union.

seceded territory: A territory viewed as having seceded from the Union. In 1861, Arizona, at the time still part of the New Mexico Territory, was referred to by some as a seceded territory.

secede from the Union, to: Of a state, to withdraw from the Union. Thomas Jefferson used the phrase hypothetically in 1825. In the 1860s it was used in earnest.

seceder: A Southerner belonging to a seceding state. Before the war, the word designated one who advocated secession.

seceding state: A state that seceded from the Union. The expression was used hypothetically by at least the 1830s.

secesh: A Northern term for a Confederate soldier or for any seceder. Also used collectively: *the secesh*.

secesh, to: To secede.

Seceshdom: The land of the secessionists. Aka *Secessia* (1) and *Secessiondom* (q.v. both).

seceshed, to get: To get separated from the Union.

secesher: A Northern term for a Southern secessionist.

seceshly: In the manner of the secessionists, as in a "seceshly inclined tavern-keeper."

Secessia: (1) The Southern Confederacy. Aka *Seceshdom* and *Secessiondom* (q.v. both). (2) A Columbia, South Carolina, bell that rang out every state as it seceded.

secession: (1) (noun) The withdrawal of a state from the Union. The word was recorded in the South by at least 1830, but its widespread use dates from the Civil War era. (2) (attributive) Pertaining to Southern secession. The word appeared in many combinations, such as *secession army*, *secession Congress*, and *secession senator*. Distinctive examples follow.

secession bread: Southern bread made with rice flour because of the shortage of wheat.

secession convention: Any of the state conventions held to consider or declare secession.

Secessiondom: The Southern Confederacy. Aka *Seceshdom* and *Secessia* (q.v. both).

secessioner: Same as *secesher* (q.v.).

secession flag: Any of the various flags adopted by seceding states or by the Confederate government.

secessionism: The principles or policies of the Southern secessionists.

secessionist: One who supported the Southern Confederacy. Before the war, one who advocated secession.

secession ordinance: Same as *ordinance of secession* (q.v.).

secession sympathizer: A Northerner in sympathy with Southern secession.

second class: See *first class*.

Secret Line: An underground spy system between Richmond and the Baltimore-Washington area, used by Confederate espionage and counterespionage agents.

seed-tick coffee: Any of various coffee substitutes in the South during the Civil War. A list would be nearly endless, but rye, bran, parched crumbs, okra seeds, and sweet potatoes were among the items used. The name reflected people's attitude toward the substitutes: seed ticks are the larvae of ticks (insects).

see the elephant, to: To experience combat. A wartime application of the expression, which, since at least the 1840s, had figuratively meant to see the sights and gain experience in life.

sergeant of the floor: In some military prisons, a noncommissioned officer elected by the prisoners.

XVII Corps Medal: An award designed by the Union corps commander James B. McPherson for the officers and men who served under him.

shadow soup: A weak chicken soup served in hospitals.

Shaler bullet: A Union .58 caliber bullet that, after firing, separated into three pieces as it flew toward the target.

Sharps rifle: A breechloading shoulder arm invented by Christian Sharps in the late 1840s and known for its range and accuracy. Sharps rifles were used by Kansas Free-Soilers in the 1850s (see also *Beecher's Bible*) and by Union troops during the Civil War.

shebang: A crude temporary shelter, made from anything available, such as brush and blankets. The term may be a variant of *shebeen*, an Irish-rooted word for a low-grade tavern.

sheep-dip: Inferior whiskey. Named after the liquid preparation for cleaning sheep.

sheep rack: A soldiers' term for a *cheval-de-frise* (q.v.). An actual sheep rack was a framework for feeding sheep.

sheet-iron cracker: A soldiers' slang term for a piece of hardtack. A related idea was expressed in *teeth-duller* (q.v.).

shell fever: Nervous paralysis just before going into battle.

shelter half: Half of a two-man *shelter tent* (q.v.), carried by a soldier and buttoned together with another soldier's half for use. Aka *half-shelter*.

shelter tent: A small wedge-shaped field tent, usually for two men, each of whom carried a *shelter half* (q.v.), that was buttoned together with another half and then pitched over a ridgepole or horizontal rope strung between vertical poles, or muskets. Aka *doghouse*, *dog tent*, *pup tent*, and *tente d'abri* (q.v. all).

Sherman's bowtie (Sherman bowtie): Same as *Sherman's hairpin* (q.v.).

Sherman's bummers: During Sherman's *March to the Sea* (q.v.), stragglers who robbed civilians and needlessly destroyed property. Some of these men were undoubtedly Sherman's own special foragers, but many were independent deserters (North and South), Federal AWOLs, and Southern civilians.

Sherman's gorillas: A term sometimes applied to the men under the Union commander William Tecumseh Sherman.

Sherman's hairpin (Sherman hairpin): A railroad rail that had been pried up, heated and softened over a bonfire of railroad ties, and then twisted around a tree till shaped like a hairpin; sometimes bent into a doughnut shape by use of railroad hooks. Railroad "hairpins" were made famous during Sherman's destructive *March to the Sea* (q.v.). Aka *iron doughnut, Jeff Davis necktie, Lincoln gimlet, Sherman's bowtie,* and *Sherman's necktie.*

Sherman's monument: Same as *Sherman's sentinel* (q.v.).

Sherman's necktie (Sherman necktie): Same as *Sherman's hairpin* (q.v.).

Sherman's sentinel: A chimney standing amid the charred remnants of a building burned down by Sherman's men during his *March to the Sea* (q.v.). Aka *Sherman's monument,* a term not common till after the war. Cf. *Kilpatrick's monument.*

shinplaster: A derisive name, North and South, for *fractional currency* (q.v.). The term had been applied to small-value or suspect currency during various earlier periods in American history. Originally, *shinplaster* had designated a small piece of paper soaked in a home remedy and plastered onto a sore leg.

shoat brands (shoat bars): A noncommissioned officer's chevrons. Since at least the early 1800s, *shoat* had meant an idle, worthless person (a spinoff on the usual sense of the word, a young pig).

shoddy: (1) An inferior woolen yarn made by combining new wool with used woolen fabrics; also, cloth made from such yarn. The word, of uncertain origin, was first applied to this material in England in the 1830s. (2) Any worthless item superficially made to look superior. Early in the Civil War, unscrupulous Federal contractors used shoddy to manufacture Union soldiers' uniforms, which quickly fell apart. Soon the word *shoddy* was being used to designate the uniforms themselves, other kinds of inferior government material, and any poorly made product. (3) A class of people who tried to pass themselves off as being superior by virtue of their (usually ill-gotten) wealth, but were in fact inferior in character and moral worth. This sense of the word was originally applied to those who made fortunes in United States contracts by supplying inferior goods. These people were such a major factor early in the war that some observers called the early 1860s "the age of shoddy." Aka *shoddy aristocracy* (q.v.).

shoddy aristocracy (shoddycracy, shoddyocracy): People who were vulgarly pretentious, especially because of new wealth. Originally said of those who cheated the United States government in Civil War contracts. Aka *shoddy* (3).

shoddyism: Pretentious vulgarity of style. Cf. *shoddy aristocracy*.

shoddyite: A person who dealt in shoddy goods; one of the shoddy class. Cf. *shoddy* (2) and (3).

shortrifle: A nickname for the Enfield rifle. So called to distinguish it from longer shoulder firearms.

shoulder strap: An officer. Northern officers wore shoulder straps bearing an insignia of rank.

show blood, to: (1) To be slightly wounded. (2) To prove the existence of a wound when retreating from combat.

shucks: Confederate paper currency. So called because, not backed by gold or silver, the notes had little real value. Shucks were corn husks, and before the war, the word *shucks* had already come to designate something worthless. See also *blueback, Confed* (2), and *grayback* (2). Cf. *greenback.*

Sibley stove: A small, portable, cone-shaped stove used in the *Sibley tent* (q.v.).

Sibley tent: A bell-shaped tent that was supported by an upright center pole and that could house ten to twenty or more soldiers, who slept with their feet to the center and their heads toward the edge. Invented in the mid-1850s by Henry Hopkins Sibley, a United States Army officer (later a Confederate) who reportedly modeled the tent on the Indian tepees he had seen when stationed in the West.

side knife: The official name for any sheath knife carried by a Confederate soldier. Aka *Arkansas toothpick* and *bowie knife* (q.v. both).

Signal Corps: The army branch in charge of communications. The *United States Army Signal Corps* was established in 1860 but not given official status till 1863. The *Confederate States Army Signal Corps* was founded in 1862.

silent battle: Same as *acoustic shadow* (q.v.).

sinker: Soldiers' slang for a piece of hardtack. During the 1860s, the term was applied to various heavy food items that would presumably sink in water or coffee, such as biscuits and dumplings. (Later, of course, the word would become most closely associated with doughnuts.)

skedaddle: An incidence of skedaddling, as in "a grand skedaddle of secesh." See *skedaddle*, to.

skedaddle (skeedadle, skiddaddle), to: (1) To retreat quickly, or flee, from the battlefield. The term was popular in the North for describing a Confederate troops' flight. The origin of the word is uncertain. It may be, as the *Oxford English Dictionary* suggests, a purely fanciful formation. But there is some evidence that it may have come from a similar Scots and English dialect verb meaning "to spill" (in fact, Americans, too, used this sense of *to skedaddle*) and the extended sense "to disperse in flight" (like milk spilling every which way). The ultimate source is probably Greek *skedannunai* ("to split up"). While its American use is said to date from the 1820s, the word was first popularized during the Civil War. (2) To run away or depart hurriedly. A generalized extension of the military sense.

skedaddler: One who skedaddles. See *skedaddle, to.*

skillygalee: (1) Hardtack pulverized, soaked in water, and fried in pork fat. The word was borrowed from British English (where the spelling was often *skilligalee* and the dish was any of various kinds of gruel). Aka *hellfire stew* (2) and *hish and hash* (2). (2) Whole hardtack soaked in water and fried in pork fat.

skirmish, to: To dig lice off one's body and out of one's clothing. A soldiers' humorous use of the old military verb meaning to engage in a small battle.

skiugle (scyugle), to: To move quickly, wildly. A short-lived expression, it was used with such specific meanings as "to run quickly toward the enemy" and "to ricochet wildly" (said of a cannonball, for example).

slavocracy (slaveocracy): A dominant or powerful class consisting of slaveholders and those favoring slavery. The term had been in use since at least 1840.

sloosh: See *slosh*.

slope, to: To desert. A military application of the verb that, since at least 1830, had meant to depart, run away (probably from the older *to slope* meaning to move in an oblique direction).

sloper: Deserter. See also *slope, to*.

slop over, to: To go to excess in speech or action, especially out of zealousness or sentimentality. This expression became popular just before the war.

slosh (sloosh): See *cush.*

slouch hat: A soft, usually felt, hat with a broad brim that tended to droop, or "slouch," over the face. The style originated in England in the 1830s, but it attained its greatest popularity when Confederate soldiers adopted it in great numbers.

slow bear: Same as *mud lark* (q.v.).

slow deer: Same as *mud lark* (q.v.).

smoked Yank (smoked Yankee): A black person, especially a soldier.

smoke pole: A nickname for any of the huge, old-fashioned shoulder firearms brought into camp by new recruits early in the war.

snake medicine: Cheap whiskey.

Snotty-Nosed Yank: The Rebels' derisive interpretation of SNY, an insignia for the State of New York, stamped on the belt plates of Yankees from New York.

Social Band: Same as *Sons of the South* (1) (q.v.).

soda-pop gun: Same as *Dahlgren* (q.v.).

soda-water bottle: Same as *Dahlgren* (q.v.).

soft duty: Duty well behind the front, especially clerical jobs.

softtack: Ordinary soft bread, as distinguished from *hard-tack* (q.v.). The term had been in use since the early 1800s.

soldiers' battle: A battle in which the leadership of the generals and commanders was minimal or nonexistent, and the outcome was determined by the initiative of the soldiers.

soldier's bulletproof vest: A type of iron vest manufactured by G. and D. Cook and Company of New Haven, Connecticut, early in the war. By 1862 most of the bulky contraptions had been tossed away or turned into frying pans.

soldiers' home: A place to stay for old or disabled soldiers. This term came into existence just before the Civil War.

soldier's letter: The two-word code that, when placed on the front of an envelope, allowed a Union soldier to mail a letter without postage. A soldier could write the words himself or use a printed envelope supplied free by the United States Christian Commission.

Somebody's Darlin': A soldiers' euphemism for a dead body, from the popular song "Somebody's Darling."

son of a seadog: (1) A dish blending everything available. Aka *hellfire stew* (1) and *hish and hash* (1). (2) *Desiccated vegetables* (q.v.), especially when boiled in a kettle.

Sons of America: A secret pro-Union society in the South.

Sons of Liberty: See *Knights of the Golden Circle*.

Sons of the South: (1) A secret society formed in 1854 by Missourians to extend slavery into Kansas and other territories. Aka *Blue Lodge, Friends Society,* and *Social Band.* (2) A semi-military group prepared to defend the South early in the war.

sound on the goose, to be: See *goose question.*

sour crout (sour kraut): Same as *sauerkraut* (q.v.).

South: The Confederate States of America and/or its population. Before the Civil War, the word had a geographical denotation, referring to the land or the people of the southern part of the United States. With the war came the political sense of the term.

Southern Confederacy: The Confederate States of America. The phrase was used to refer to a contemplated confederacy as early as 1788.

Southern Cross: The *Battle Flag* (q.v.) of the Southern Confederacy.

Southern Empire: The Southern Confederacy.

Southernism: The qualities characteristic of Southern life or culture. The term gained currency during the Civil War.

Southern league: Any of the military leagues (organizations) established in the South early in the war.

Southern Manifesto: A declaration drawn up by two Southern senators, signed by twenty-nine other Southern lawmakers (six senators and twenty-three congressmen), and issued on December 14, 1860, stating that Congress had reached an impasse and that the formation of a Southern Confederacy was necessary.

Southern Union man: A Southern man who favored the Union in the Civil War.

sowbelly: Pork, especially salt pork.

spar torpedo: An explosive device attached to the end of a long pole (spar) at the bow of a warship and rammed into an enemy vessel. At least one kind of spar torpedo was not rammed but was released far enough underwater so that it would float up to the target. See also *torpedo*.

Spencer: An important Union repeating carbine and rifle with a seven-shot magazine, designed by Christopher M. Spencer just before the Civil War.

Spencer saddle: A saddle patented in 1862 by Robert Spencer of Brooklyn. It was designed with front pieces that prevented the rider from being thrown forward over the saddle.

spike, to: To disable (a muzzleloading cannon) by driving a spike into the vent. The term had been in use since the seventeenth century.

spill skull: A Southern term for contraband liquor.

spoiled darling: Same as *carpet knight* (2) (q.v.).

spoon, to: To sleep close together with others in a spoon formation, with knees drawn up. Soldiers often had to sleep in spoon fashion because their tents were so crowded. To change positions in such tight quarters, a soldier would yell, "Spoon!" Everyone rolled over at the same time.

sporting house: A gambling house or brothel.

Springfield: A standard rifle on both sides during the Civil War. Named after the government armory in Springfield, Massachusetts, the shoulder arm was issued in 1861, 1863, and 1864 models.

Stainless Banner: Same as *National Flag, Confederate* (q.v.).

stake torpedo: See *torpedo*.

stamp: Same as *postage stamp* (q.v.).

stamped notes: Paper money issued with revenue or other stamps attached to add to the face value or to validate the notes.

stamp money: Postage and other (e.g., revenue) stamps serving as *fractional currency* (q.v.). Legalized on July 17, 1862, but commonly used long before then. These were actual stamps (at first, regular gummed stamps, later ungummed stamps printed on heavier paper to withstand extra handling), not to be confused with the reproductions in *postage currency* (q.v.).

stamps: Money, especially paper currency of any denomination(s). The term was a slang extension of the more narrow sense of *stamps* as a simple plural of *stamp* (q.v.) in its money senses.

standard: A unit flag flown by cavalrymen. The term had long been used for various flags in England and America. Cf. *color* (1) and *ensign* (1).

standard-bearer: A soldier who carried a unit's *standard* (q.v.). Cf. *color-bearer*.

Stars and Bars: The first flag of the Confederacy, adopted in early 1861. In the upper left corner was a blue field on which were seven white stars in a circle; the rest of the flag consisted of two horizontal red bars separated by a white one. On the battlefield, this flag could not always be distinguished from the Union's Stars and Stripes, so later in 1861 the Confederacy created the *Battle Flag* (q.v.), which is often erroneously referred to as the Stars and Bars. See also *National Flag, Confederate*.

Star-spangled fever: The early wave of Union patriotism as characterized by the frequent displaying of the flag and playing of "The Star-spangled Banner."

state line: The military force of a state enrolled for combat service. The term was established before the war.

stay-at-home ranger: A man not fighting in the war.

stock: A band of stiff leather fastened about the neck, probably to make the soldier hold his head up. Rarely actually worn. The term had been in civilian uses since at least the early 1700s.

stockade, to: To place a wedge or shelter tent on top of a log base for extra protection from the elements. The term was generally used in a participial form: "stockaded tent." Aka *to barricade* (*barricaded*) and *to winterize* (*winterized*).

stone fence: A mixed alcoholic drink, especially whiskey and cider. The term had been in use since at least the early 1840s.

stone fleet: A group of old ships that Union forces, to help implement their blockade of Confederate ports, loaded with stones and scuttled at the entrances to Southern harbors.

strawfoot: See *hayfoot, strawfoot*.

stray: A Union soldiers' tongue-in-cheek term for a domestic hog or fowl that they had stolen.

Street, the: Already, in 1863, a nickname for Wall Street as the financial capital of the United States.

striker: A soldier who did odd jobs for an officer. The term was borrowed from civilian use, where it had long designated various kinds of workers.

stumptail: At the beginning of the war, a term for a bank note secured by a Southern state bond or for any depreciated Northern issue; both were circulated at discounts.

The word was a specific application of *stumptail* meaning anything damaged or inferior.

subgenation: The subjection of one race to another. The word was coined by J. H. Van Evrie in his 1864 writing entitled *Subgenation: The Theory of the Normal Relation of the Races; an Answer to "Miscegenation."* *Subgenation* is based on a combination of Latin roots meaning "the subjection of a race." Cf. *miscegenation*.

subsistence stores: Supplies of food and other items to support military personnel.

substitute: Someone hired to replace a drafted man. The term had had a similar meaning since the days of the revolutionary war.

substitute broker: A person who, for a fee, would find substitutes for drafted men wanting to avoid military service.

subtle poison: Coffee.

Sucker: A soldier from Illinois. The word had been a nickname for an Illinoisan since at least the 1830s.

sudden death: Cheap whiskey.

sutler: A civilian who sold provisions to soldiers in the field or in garrison. The term had been so used since the late sixteenth century.

sutler note: A private scrip issued by a sutler.

sutler pie: A popular pastry sold by sutlers.

Swamp Angel: The large Parrott rifle used by the Union commander Quincy A. Gillmore to shell Charleston, South Carolina, from nearby swamps in 1863. Before the Civil War, the term *swamp angel* had designated a person who lived in, or was familiar with, swamps. The projectile fired by the gun was called a *nigger baby* (q.v.).

swap horses while crossing the river (swap horses while crossing a stream), to: To change a leader in a crisis, or ideas or plans in the middle of a project. The expression was, and is, nearly always stated in the negative. It was popularized when Abraham Lincoln used it in an address in 1864 after being renominated to the presidency: "I do not allow myself to suppose that either the Convention or the League have concluded to decide that I am either the greatest or best man in America, but rather they have concluded that it is not best to swap horses while crossing the river, and have further concluded that I am not so poor a horse that they might not make a botch of it in trying to swap." The exact wording of Lincoln's expression was variously recorded by contemporaries. Later versions included *to change horses in midstream*.

swift: A flying bullet.

swing off, to: To desert to another side.

T

T: An abbreviation for *thief* (or *thievery*). The letter was stamped with indelible ink, or burned with a red-hot iron, onto the hip, hand, cheek, or forehead of an offender.

take a French (take French leave), to: See *French leave*.

take a twist at the tiger, to: See *tiger*.

tanglefoot (tangleleg): Inferior whiskey.

tanyard: A Yankee name for a broad army shoe. The word conjured up the image of a large tanning vat in a tannery.

taps: The last call at night, signaling lights out. The word had been used with this meaning since the early 1800s. However, the modern bugle tune known as taps originated in 1862 when the Union general Daniel Butterfield, with help from a bugler, adapted the *tattoo* (q.v.) call into a new piece. Previously a French call had been used for lights out.

tarantula juice: Cheap whiskey.

tar bucket: Slang for a tall *kepi* (q.v.).

Tarheel: A nickname for a soldier from North Carolina. The state had long been known for its production of tar and pitch, which presumably would stick to the heels of people who lived and worked around such material. The term was apparently firmly established before the circulation of the well-known story about North Carolinians running from a battle because they had "forgotten to tar their heels that morning."

tattoo: The call signaling soldiers to go to their quarters at night. The word had been used with this meaning since the early 1600s. Originally the call was a drumbeat, but later it became a bugle call. During the Civil War, the bugler played a call that had been officially used since at least 1835. See also *taps*.

teeth-duller: A soldiers' slang term for a piece of hardtack. A related idea was expressed in *sheet-iron cracker* (q.v.).

ten acres and a mule: See *forty acres and a mule*.

tenement: A soldiers' term for their winter quarters. The word was borrowed from civilian use, where it designated an apartment house for poor people and was, in the late 1850s, just beginning to gain currency.

ten forty: A popular name for a type of United States government bond issued in 1864, redeemable after ten years and payable in forty years.

Tennessee Tory: A Confederate name for a Tennessee Unionist who joined the Northern army.

Tennessee quickstep: See *quickstep*. Aka *Tennessee trots and Tennessee two-step*.

tente d'abri: French for *shelter tent* (q.v.).

tent peg: A slang term for a bayonet, which was so seldom used in combat that soldiers commonly named it and used it as a tent peg and a *candlestick* (q.v.).

Thanks of Congress: A formal congressional acknowledgment of wartime service. In the North, these tributes focused on army and navy personnel, and only a small number were given. In the South, however, many such resolutions were passed for officers, military and naval units, civilians, and even entire states.

third class: See *first class*.

$300 man: A derisive term among early Union volunteers for those who volunteered later in the war, when bounties had risen to $300 for three-year men.

three-month: Enlisted for three months, as in "three-month volunteers." Such men were often mistreated by other soldiers.

ticket to Dixie: A draft call for a Northerner.

tiger: The game of faro, popular among soldiers during the Civil War. This nickname was recorded by at least the 1830s. *To buck* (or *fight*) the tiger was to play against the bank or, more broadly, to play cards of any kind or gamble in any way. To join a gambling game was *to take a twist at the tiger*.

timberclad: A wooden warship protected by extra layers of hard timbers. Timberclads were mainly used as river gunboats, especially early in the war before iron plating became common.

tin can on a shingle: Same as *cheesebox* (q.v.).

tinclad: A gunboat protected with light armor. The armor consisted of thin iron plates, not tin. The word *tin* was used to distinguish the vessels from the more heavily plated *ironclad* (q.v.) type. Tinclads generally operated in shallow rivers and lakes, and the armor was designed mostly for protection from small-arms fire. Aka *light draft*.

tintype: A photograph taken as a positive on a thin plate of tin. Patented in the mid-1850s, the process became popular during the Civil War. The expression *not on your tintype* ("certainly not") probably originated during this period, though the earliest published evidence dates from a few years later.

toothpick: Short for *Arkansas toothpick* (q.v.).

torpedo: A mine, land or marine. The term had been in use since the late 1700s. Americans used a wide variety of torpedoes in the Civil War, such as a *kep torpedo* (in a keg) and a *stake torpedo* (at the end of a stake). For special types, see *coal torpedo, horological torpedo, spar torpedo*, and *torpedo raft*.

torpedo raft: A raft of several logs with cast-iron torpedoes attached, anchored below the surface. See also torpedo.

Tory: Same as *homegrown Yankee* (q.v.). During the American Revolution, the word had designated someone loyal to the British.

Tower of London musket: An old musket left over from the War of 1812 (against the British, hence the name) and used by some troops in the Civil War.

transfugee: A term sometimes used to designate a *galvanized* (q.v.) soldier. The word was probably an Americanism coined during the Civil War and based on a blending of *trans-* (as in "transfer" of loyalty) and *refugee*. But the word *transfuge*, though rare and by the 1860s nearly obsolete, had long meant a deserter in British English.

trappings (traps): A soldier's possessions. The term had been in civilian use since the late 1500s to mean external embellishments.

Treasury greenback: Same as *greenback* (q.v.).

tub: An artillery missile.

turpentine: Inferior liquor of various kinds. Often used attributively, as in *turpentine gin, turpentine spirits,* and *turpentine whiskey.* This slang sense of the word went back at least to the 1770s.

turtle: An *ironclad* (q.v.) having an upper deck that suggested a turtle's back.

Twenty-Negro Law (Twenty-Nigger Law, Twenty-Slave Law): The provision in the Confederate conscription laws of 1862 that exempted from military service the overseer or owner of any plantation with twenty or more slaves. Later the number was lowered to fifteen, generating the expressions *Fifteen-Negro Law*, *Fifteen-Nigger Law*, and *Fifteen-Slave Law*.

two-cent piece: A bronze coin issued by the Union government in 1864. It was the first United States coin to bear the inscription "In God We Trust."

tycoon: A top leader. Abraham Lincoln and Robert E. Lee were so called by the people close to them. The word was adapted from Japanese *taikun* ("great ruler, military leader"), the title by which the shogun of Japan was described to foreigners. Its extension to business magnates came after the war.

U

Uncle Lincoln's Asses: A copperhead interpretation of the abbreviation ULA (*Union League of America* [q.v.]).

Uncle Sam's pigpen: A Northern soldiers' term for an army camp, notably Camp Curtin.

Uncle Sam's webfeet: The American navy. The term had been in use since at least the 1840s.

unconditional surrender: Surrender without condition or stipulation. The expression became familiar in America in 1862 when General Grant, upon being asked by the commander of Fort Donelson (in Tennessee) for surrender conditions, replied that only "unconditional and immediate surrender" would be accepted. Soon U.S. Grant became known as Unconditional Surrender Grant. The term, however, had been recorded in British English by at least the 1840s.

unconditional Union man: In the campaign of 1864, a supporter of the administration and a member of the National Union party, whose goal was "the unconditional maintenance of the Union." Cf. *Union man*.

Unfortunate Soldiers Sadly Sold: A humorous interpretation of the abbreviation U.S.S.S. (United States Sharpshooters) by the sharpshooters themselves.

Union: (1) (noun) The Northern states. The word had been used as early as the 1750s in discussions about a possible joining of the colonies. (2) (adjective) Pertaining to, or loyal to, the United States or the Union cause. Union loyalties versus "states' rights" leanings were already being recorded by at least the 1830s. During the Civil War, the word appeared in many combinations, such as *Union army*, *Union people*, and *Union soldier*. Distinctive examples follow.

Union anaconda: Same as *anaconda* (q.v.).

Union cause: The Northern or Federal cause curing the Civil War.

Union flag: The flag of the United States, i.e., the Stars and Stripes. The term had been used during the revolutionary war to designate the flag of the federated colonies.

Union gun: Same as *Ager gun* (q.v.).

Unionism: Allegiance to the Union.

Unionist: (1) (noun) A supporter of the Union side in the Civil War. The term had designated a person loyal to the Federal Union since at least the 1830s. (2) (adjective) Loyal to the Union cause.

Union League of America: See *loyal league*.

Union man: A Northern sympathizer. Before the Civil War, the term had referred more broadly to anyone who placed loyalty to the Federal Union above loyalty to a state or other region. Cf. *unconditional Union man*.

Union party: A coalition of Republicans and War Democrats against the Peace Democrats. Aka *National Union party*.

Union repeating gun: Same as *Ager gun* (q.v.).

Union ticket: The ticket of the Constitutional Union party or of any one of various other parties supporting the Union. Before the war, the term had designated a ticket that included candidates of different political views.

United States Army Signal Corps: See *Signal Corps*.

United States Christian Commission: See *Christian Commission*.

United States Military Telegraph: See *Military Telegraph*.

United States Regular Army: See *Regular Army, United States*.

United States Sanitary Commission: See *Sanitary Commission*.

universal scout: A double agent, i.e., a spy serving one side while pretending to serve the other.

U.S. Volunteer: See *galvanized*.

V

Vallandighamer: An Ohio term for a Southern sympathizer. Clement L. Vallandigham was a well-known Ohio politician who was arrested for treason and, in 1863, banished by President Lincoln to the Confederacy. (Vallandigham sneaked back into the United States in 1864.)

veal: An experienced soldiers' name for a new recruit.

vedette (vidette): A mounted sentry. The word, borrowed from French in the late seventeenth century, is based on a Latin root meaning "to watch."

veteranize, to: To reenlist as a soldier. Said of a Union soldier whose original three-year term was expiring in 1864 and who reenlisted to receive a bounty, a furlough, and a special status as a *veteran volunteer*.

Veteran Reserve Corps: See *Invalid Corps* (q.v.).

veteran volunteer: See *veteranize, to*.

vice admiral: See *admiral*.

vidette: Same as *vedette* (q.v.).

Virginia quickstep: See *quickstep*.

vivandière: A woman who followed a camp and performed such functions as cooking and nursing. The masculine form of the word, *vivandier*, was borrowed from French in the sixteenth century and meant "a sutler" (the word is based on a Medieval Latin word for "food"), so that the original European sense of vivandière was "a female sutler."

V.O.P.: A symbol used on bottles of brandy intended for Union officers. The abbreviation stood for *Very Old Pale*, a reference to the age of the liquor.

W

W: An abbreviation for *worthless* or (*worthlessness*). The letter was stamped with indelible ink, or burned with a red-hot iron, onto the hip, hand, cheek, or forehead of an offender.

Wade-Davis Bill: A stringent Reconstruction bill passed by Congress in 1864 but pocket vetoed by President Lincoln.

Wade-Davis Manifesto: A *New York Tribune* article (summer 1864) that criticized President Lincoln for pocket vetoing the *Wade-Davis Bill* (q.v.) and thus usurping congressional authority in the matter of Reconstruction.

wagon dog: A Confederate soldier who, to avoid battle, pretended to be ill and dropped back to the wagon trains.

wallpaper edition: An edition of a Mississippi newspaper, the *Vicksburg Daily Citizen*, brought out on wallpaper during the siege of 1863.

wall tent: A tent shaped like a small house, with four perpendicular walls. The term had been in use since at least the 1840s. The structure was sometimes used as a hospital, in which case it was also called a *hospital tent* (q.v.).

war correspondence: The reports from a *war correspondent* (q.v.).

war correspondent: A journalist who traveled with an army and reported war news from the front. The term was recorded by Charles Dickens in 1844, but its common use in America dates from the Civil War. Aka *battle correspondent*.

war crop: A crop calculated to meet wartime needs, such as potatoes.

War Democracy: Collectively, the War Democrats. See also *War Democrat*.

War Democrat: A Northern member of the Democratic party who supported Lincoln's administration.

war governor: A governor of a state during the Civil War.

war hotel: A soldiers' term for a place of confinement for prisoners of war.

warrant officers' champagne: Grog mixed with ginger ale.

war widow: A woman whose husband was away in military service.

war will be over by Christmas, the: A popular saying early in the Civil War.

Washingtonia: A name suggested for the Confederacy in 1860.

Washington pie: Hardtack pulverized, mixed in water, formed into a thin cake, and baked.

water soldier: A marine.

water walker: One of two small watertight canoes worn on the feet of a soldier so that he could "walk" across a river, additionally aided by a paddle for balance and propulsion. This equipment was proposed by adherents in the Union in 1861 and 1863 but was never mass-produced.

wayside: A home for ailing soldiers, operated by volunteers in the South.

webfoot: An infantryman.

wedge tent: Same as *A tent* (q.v.).

weevil fodder: Soldiers' slang for hardtack, known for housing small creatures. Cf. *worm castle*.

whang: A soldiers' slang term for an army shoe. *Whang* was an old word for a thong (leather strap).

wheel, to: Of a line of troops, to pivot on one end while the rest of the line swung around like the spoke of a wheel, changing direction but retaining the linear formation. The command had been in use since the sixteenth century.

Whipple hat: A light-blue felt hat with a brim running around the back and sides, while a leather visor covered the front. Patented in 1861 by J.F. Whipple of New York. Known to Confederates as the *Excelsior hat*.

Whistling Dick: An eighteen-pounder cannon used by the Confederates at Vicksburg. Its rifling gave its projectiles an erratic spin, which produced a whistling sound while in flight.

white-oak chip: Soldiers' slang for a piece of hardtack. Wood from the white-oak tree is noted for its toughness.

white Republican: A white person in the Republican party, as distinguished from the many blacks who entered the party during, and just after, the Civil War.

whitewashed Rebel: See *galvanized*.

Who wouldn't be a soldier?: A soldiers' sarcastic expression meaning "Who cares?"

Wide-awake: A supporter of Abraham Lincoln, usually young and faintly military. The term originated in the 1860 campaign.

will fits: A feigned illness by malingerers. The main "symptoms" were writhing in pain and frothing (faked with soap) at the mouth.

Williams rapid-fire gun: A Confederate hand-cranked, rapid-firing, breech-loading artillery piece invented by R.S. Williams. First manufactured in 1861. It was nicknamed the *Confederate secret weapon*.

Winans' steam gun: A boiler-operated weapon allegedly able to project missiles of any size, from a bullet to a hundred-pound cannonball. Invented by Charles Dickinson and manufactured by Ross Winans in Baltimore. It was captured by the Federals in May 1861 and was never fired in battle.

winterize, to: Same as *stockade, to* (q.v.).

wire entanglement: An obstacle of wire stretched over the ground, usually between trees, to trip and stall the enemy.

Woman Order: The proclamation issued on May 15, 1862, by Benjamin F. Butler, Union commander in occupied New Orleans, to curtail the insults hurled at Union personnel by New Orleans women. Any female who insulted a Federal officer or soldier would be "treated as a woman of the town plying her avocation," i.e., a prostitute. The harassment of the Northerners virtually ended.

woman's aid society (women's-aid society): A *Ladies' Aid Society* (q.v.).

worm a bullet, to: To remove an unfired bullet from a muzzleloading gun by attaching a worm (a screw device) to the end of a ramrod, inserting it down the gun barrel, screwing it into the bullet, and then removing the projectile.

worm castle: Hardtack with worms in it. Cf. *weevil fodder*.

wristbreaker: A heavy cavalry saber issued to troops. Aka *old wristbreaker*.

Y

yaller dog: A Confederate infantrymen's term for a young staff officer who served as an aide to senior officers.

Yank: Short for *Yankee* (q.v.). This form was being recorded by at least 1778.

Yankee: A Northerner, especially a Union soldier. The origin of the term is uncertain, but the earliest recorded evidence in English shows the word as a personal nickname for a Dutchman, as in "Yankey Duch [Dutch]" (1683); so the word probably comes from Dutch *Janke*, a diminutive of *Jan* ("John"). Because of its widespread use as a personal nickname in New England, *Yankee*, by the mid-1700s, came to designate any New Englander or, more generally, any Northerner; British soldiers and Southerners often uttered the word derisively. Then, during the Revolutionary War, the British applied the word to all Americans.

Yankee bummer: A Union soldier who became a *bummer* (2) (q.v.).

Yankee cheesebox on a raft: Same as *cheesebox* (q.v.).

Yankeedom: The realm of the Yankees. The term was in use by at least the 1830s.

Yankee Doodle: A Yankee, especially a Union soldier; Yankees collectively; or the whole North. The term, in use since at least 1770, came from "Yankee Doodle," a popular song just before and during the American Revolution.

Yankee Doodledom: The realm of the Yankee Doodles. The term was in use by at least the 1840s.

Yankee grit: The persevering courage of Yankees.

Yankee seven-devils: A Confederate soldiers' term for the Union's Spencer repeating rifle, which had a seven-shot magazine.

Yellowhammer: A nickname for a Confederate soldier from Alabama. Alabamians sometimes wore uniforms made with a homemade dye of a yellowish hue. *Yellowhammer* is the name of a familiar yellow-colored bird.

Young Bloods of the South: Young Southern military leaders characterized by boldness, bravery, and a natural instinct for war. The term was coined by William Tecumseh Sherman. One of the men he had in mind was Nathan Bedford Forrest.

Z

Zouave: A member of any North or South volunteer unit that adopted the colorful dress and precision drill of the French Zouaves. The French infantry units so named were originally composed of Algerians (*Zouave* is based on the name of an Algerian tribe), but later of Frenchmen who imitated the Algerians in their brilliant uniforms and snappy drill. The French units originated in the 1830s and toured the United States just before the Civil War, thus inspiring the formation of similar units in America.

Zou-Zou: A nickname for *Zouave* (q.v.).

Zu-Zu: A nickname for *Zouave* (q.v.).

Selected Bibliography

Adams, Ramon F. *Western Words: A Dictionary of the American West.* Rev. ed. Norman: University of Oklahoma Press, 1968.

Annals of America, The. Vol. 9, 1858-1865: The Crisis of the Union. Chicago: Encyclopaedia Britannica, 1968.

Billings, John D. *Hardtack and Coffee; or, The Unwritten Story of Army Life.* Boston: George M. Smith and Co., 1887.

Boatner, Mark Mayo, III. *The Civil War Dictionary.* Rev. ed. New York: David McKay Co., 1988.

Boeger, Palmer H. "Hardtack and Burned Beans." *Civil War History,* March 1958, pp. 73-92.

Cannon, Devereaux D. *Flags of the Confederacy: An Illustrated History.* Memphis: St. Lukes Press and Broadfoot Publishing, 1988.

Carman, W.Y. *A Dictionary of Military Uniform.* New York: Charles Scribner's Sons, 1977.

Cassidy, Frederic G., ed. Vols. 1-2. *Dictionary of American Regional English.* Cambridge, Mass.: Harvard University Press, Belknap Press, 1985, 1991.

Catton, Bruce. *The Centennial History of the Civil War.* 3 vols. Garden City, N.Y.: Doubleday and Co., 1961, 1963, 1965.

———. *The Civil War.* New York: Fairfax Press, 1971.

Chapman, Robert L., ed. *New Dictionary of American Slang.* New York: Harper and Row, 1986.

Clapin, Sylva. *A New Dictionary of Americanisms.* c. 1902. Reprint. Detroit: Gale Research Co., 1968.

Coggins, Jack. *Arms and Equipment of the Civil War.* New York: The Fairfax Press, 1962.

Commager, Henry Steele, ed. *The Blue and the Gray: The Story of the Civil War as Told by the Participants.* 1950. Reprint. New York: Fairfax Press, 1982.

Commager, Henry Steele, and Cantor, Milton, eds. *Documents of American History.* 10th ed. Vol. 1. Englewood Cliffs, N.J.: Prentice-Hall, 1988.

Craigie, Sir William A., and Hulbert, James R., eds. *A Dictionary of American English on Historical Principles.* 4 vols. Chicago: University of Chicago Press, 1938.

Davis, William C. *The Fighting Men of the Civil War.* New York: W.H. Smith Publishers, Gallery Books, 1989.

Dictionary of American History. Rev. ed. 8 vols. New York: Charles Scribner's Sons, 1978.

Dupuy, Trevor N.; Johnson, Curt; and Hayes, Grace P. *Dictionary of Military Terms: A Guide to the Language of Warfare and Military Institutions*. New York: The H.W. Wilson Co., 1986.

Elting, John R.; Cragg, Dan; and Deal, Ernest L. *A Dictionary of Soldier Talk*. New York: The Scribner Press, 1984.

Farmer, John S. *Americanisms—Old and New: A Dictionary of Words, Phrases, and Colloquialisms*. London: Thomas Poulter and Sons, 1889.

Faust, Patricia L., ed. *Historical Times Illustrated Encyclopedia of the Civil War*. New York: Harper and Row, Publishers, 1986.

Flexner, Stuart Berg. *I Hear America Talking*. New York: Van Nostrand Reinhold Co., 1976.

———. *Listening to America*. New York: Simon and Schuster, 1982.

Foote, Shelby. *The Civil War: A Narrative*. 3 vols. New York: Random House, Vintage Books, 1958, 1963, 1974.

Fowler, William M., Jr. *Under Two Flags: The American Navy in the Civil War*. New York: W.W. Norton and Co., 1990.

Gragg, Rod. *The Civil War Quiz and Fact Book*. New York: Harper and Row, 1985.

———. *The Illustrated Confederate Reader*. New York: Harper and Row, 1989.

Guernsey, Alfred H., and Alden, Henry M. *Harper's Pictorial History of the Great Rebellion in the United States*. 1866. Reprint. New York: The Fairfax Press, 1977.

Hessler, Gene. *The Comprehensive Catalog of U.S. Paper Money*. 4th ed. Port Clinton, Ohio: BNR Press, 1983.

Howell, Edgar M. *United States Army Headgear, 1855-1902: Catalog of United States Army Uniforms in the Collections of the Smithsonian Institution, II. Smithsonian Studies in History and Technology, no. 30*. Washington, D.C.: Superintendent of Documents, 1975.

Jordan, Robert Paul. *The Civil War*. Washington, D.C.: National Geographic Society, 1969.

Katcher, Philip. *The American Civil War Source Book*. London: Arms and Armour Press, 1992.

Krause, Chester L., and Lemke, Robert F. *Standard Catalog of United States Paper Money*. 11th ed. Edited by Robert E. Wilhite. Iola, Wis.: Krause Publications, 1992.

Leckie, Robert. *The Wars of America*. Rev. ed. New York: Harper and Row, 1981.

Lord, Francis A. *Civil War Collector's Encyclopedia*. Harrisburg, Pa.: The Stackpole Co., 1963.

————. *Civil War Collector's Encyclopedia: Military Matériel, Both American and Foreign Used by the Union and the Confederacy*. Vol. 2. W. Columbia, S.C.: Lord Americana and Research, 1975.

————. *Civil War Sutlers and Their Wares*. New York: Thomas Yoseloff, 1969.

————. *Uniforms of the Civil War*. A.S. Barnes, 1970.

Lovette, Leland P. Naval Customs, Traditions, and Usage. Annapolis, Md.: United States Naval Institute, 1939.

McCarthy, Carlton. *Detailed Minutiae of Soldier Life in the Army of Northern Virginia, 1861-1865*. Richmond, Va.: C. McCarthy and Co., 1882.

Macdonald, John. *Great Battles of the Civil War*. New York: Macmillan Publishing Co., 1988.

McPherson, James M., ed. *Battle Chronicles of the Civil War*. 6 vols. New York: Macmillan Publishing Co., 1989.

Mathews, Mitford M. *A Dictionary of Americanisms on Historical Principles*. 2 vols. Chicago: The University of Chicago Press, 1951.

Mencken, H.L. *The American Language*. 4th ed. New York: Alfred A. Knopf, 1936.

————. *The American Language*. Supp. 1. New York: Alfred A. Knopf, 1945.

————. *The American Language*. Supp. 2. New York: Alfred A. Knopf, 1948.

Miller, Nathan. *The U.S. Navy: An Illustrated History*. New York: American Heritage Publishing Co., and Annapolis, Md.: United States Naval Institute Press, 1977.

Miller, William J. *The Training of an Army: Camp Curtin and the North's Civil War*. Shippensburg, Pa.: White Mane Publishing Co., 1990.

Mitchell, Reid. *Civil War Soldiers*. New York: Viking Penguin, 1988.

Monaghan, Jay. "Civil War Slang and Humor." *Civil War History*, June 1957, pp. 125-33.

Official Records of the Union and Confederate Navies in the War of the Rebellion. Washington, D.C.: United States Government Printing Office, 1894-1927.

Oxford English Dictionary, The. 2d ed. 20 vols. Prepared by J.A. Simpson and E.S.C. Weiner. Oxford: Clarendon Press, 1989.

Pick, Albert. *Standard Catalog of World Paper Money*. 2 vols. 6th ed. Edited by Neil Shafer and Colin R. Bruce II. Iola, Wis.: Krause Publications, 1990.

Potter, E.B. *Illustrated History of the United States Navy*. New York: Galahad Books, 1971.

Quick, John. *Dictionary of Weapons and Military Terms*. New York: McGraw-Hill Book Co., 1973.

Robertson, James I., Jr. *Soldiers Blue and Gray*. Columbia, S.C.: University of South Carolina Press, 1988.

Roller, David C., and Twyman, Robert W., eds. *The Encyclopedia of Southern History*. Baton Rouge: Louisiana State University Press, 1979.

Sutherland, Daniel E. *The Expansion of Everyday Life, 1860-1876*. New York: Harper and Row, 1989.

Thomas, Dianne Stine, ed. *Brother Against Brother: Time-Life Books History of the Civil War*. New York: Prentice Hall Press, 1990.

Thornton, Richard H. *An American Glossary*. 3 vols. 1912. Reprint. 3 vols. Vol. 3 edited by Louise Hanley. New York: Frederick Ungar Publishing Co., 1962.

Urwin, Gregory J.W. *The United States Cavalry: An Illustrated History*. Poole, Dorset, England: Blandford Press, 1983.

Ward, Geoffrey C.; Burns, Ric; and Burns, Ken. *The Civil War: An Illustrated History*. New York: Alfred A. Knopf, 1990.

War of the Rebellion, The: A Compilation of the Official Records of the Union and Confederate Armies. Washington, D.C.: United States Government Printing Office, 1880-1901.

Watts, Peter. *A Dictionary of the Old West, 1850-1900*. New York: Alfred A. Knopf, 1977.

Welsh, Douglas. *The Civil War: A Complete Military History*. New York: Promontory Press, 1981.

Wiley, Bell Irvin. *The Life of Billy Yank: The Common Soldier of the Union*. Baton Rouge: Louisiana State University Press, 1952, 1971.

————. *The Life of Johnny Reb: The Common Soldier of the Confederacy*. Baton Rouge: Louisiana State University Press, 1943, 1971, 1978.

————. *They Who Fought Here*. New York: Bonanza Books, 1959.

Wilkinson, Warren. *Mother, May You Never See the Sights I Have Seen: The Fifty Seventh Massachusetts Veteran Volunteers in the Army of the Potomac, 1864-1865*. New York, Harper and Row, 1990.

Windrow, Martin, and Embleton, Gerry. *Military Dress of North America, 1665-1970*. New York: Charles Scribner's Sons, 1973.